# Jewish West Hartford

# Jewish West Hartford

From City to Suburb

Betty N. Hoffman

Charleston  London
History
PRESS

Published by The History Press
Charleston, SC 29403
www.historypress.net

Copyright © 2007 by Betty N. Hoffman
All rights reserved

*Cover Image:* Downtown Hartford circa 1900.

First published 2007

Manufactured in the United Kingdom

ISBN 978.1.59629.204.8

Library of Congress Cataloging-in-Publication Data

Hoffman, Betty N.
 Jewish West Hartford : from city to suburb / Betty N. Hoffman.
   p. cm.
 Includes bibliographical references and index.
 ISBN-13: 978-1-59629-204-8 (alk. paper)
  1. Jews--Connecticut--West Hartford--History. 2. Jews--Connecticut--West Hartford--Social life and customs. 3. Jews--Connecticut--West Hartford--Politics and government. 4. West Hartford (Conn.)--Ethnic relations. 5. Hoffman, Betty N. I. Title.
 F104.H3H642 2007
 974.6'2--dc22
                                            2007018296

*Notice*: The information in this book is true and complete to the best of our knowledge. It is offered without guarantee on the part of the author or The History Press. The author and The History Press disclaim all liability in connection with the use of this book.

All rights reserved. No part of this book may be reproduced or transmitted in any form whatsoever without prior written permission from the publisher except in the case of brief quotations embodied in critical articles and reviews.

# Contents

|  |  |  |
|---|---|---|
|  | Preface | 7 |
| Introduction | Early Settlement | 11 |
| Chapter One | Moving West | 23 |
| Chapter Two | The Pioneer Synagogues | 43 |
| Chapter Three | "It got so we all moved out—all of us." | 59 |
| Chapter Four | Community Service Agencies | 77 |
| Chapter Five | Social Structure | 96 |
|  | Notes | 123 |
|  | About the Author | 127 |

# Preface

*West Hartford has always been a very solid, middle-class community with everything good and everything not so good that that involves. Family is very important. Education is very important. Faith is very important. Support your community, the arts as long as they are not too cutting edge. West Hartford is a quintessential place to raise your children, to educate them, and to lead a relatively uncomplicated life. West Hartford's economic, commercial, professional base is expanding. A lot of this, of course, is Hartford's loss.*

*Nan Glass, former mayor and town clerk*

Although West Hartford is technically a suburb of Hartford and was within the Hartford's original boundaries until 1854, West Hartford has become an independent town, offering a pleasant alternative to city life, but with Hartford's resources only a few minutes away. Known for its exemplary schools, high level of public services, and New England charm, West Hartford has drawn new residents to its varied neighborhoods for decades. Since 1950, when the Jews began to flow out of Hartford in increasing numbers, the population has jumped from approximately forty-four thousand to slightly over sixty-one thousand.

Although it is common knowledge that the population of West Hartford is relatively evenly divided among Protestants, Catholics and Jews, Ira M. Seshkin's Jewish Community Study Summary report to the Jewish Federation of Greater Hartford in 2000 estimated the total number of Jews in this region to be about 34,377—with 15,554 living in the core area, primarily West Hartford. The core area also includes Bloomfield, the few remaining

# Preface

Jews in Hartford, college students, and those living in institutions—mainly the Hebrew Home and Hospital—and is considerably lower than the one-third estimate, but much higher than the approximately 4 percent of the entire Hartford County population. Even so, the percentage of Jews exceeds that of many other places.

When we moved to West Hartford in 1975, we intended to stay for two years, but we found the community to be as Nan Glass describes it, filled with solid values of family, education and faith—all in all a good place to make a home. In addition to simply living in West Hartford, as an anthropologist and oral historian, I have been studying the various aspects of Jewish life in Greater Hartford for more than twenty years.

In this study, I have used the traditional anthropological approach of living in a community and talking to the people around me and have combined this with the interviewing techniques of the oral historian. I have collected life stories, interviewed people about particular places or events and even recorded an accordion performance. Several individuals preferred to write the histories of their synagogues or schools, which provided me with an unexpected, but very important, resource.

The archives of the Jewish Historical of Greater Hartford Society (JHSGH) and of the Noah Webster House and West Hartford Historical Society (NWH/WHHS) are treasure troves. Without the help of the historians and archivists who dug into their files to find the perfect photographs for me, I would not have been able to put together this history. In particular, I would like to thank executive director Estelle Kafer, archivist Margaret Mair and project manager Bea Brody of the JHSGH. All photographs not otherwise identified come from their archives.

Thanks also go to executive director Chris Dobbs and archivist Sheila Daley of the NWH/WHHS. They provided photographs and technical assistance. An enormous thank you goes to all of those who opened their lives to me, showed me their albums and treasures and loaned me photographs. They are the heart of this book.

I have noted the sources for the archival interviews and for the written materials I used in the preparation of this book. If a quotation does not have a note, it is from one of those interviews I conducted and is on file at the JHSGH. Since oral histories are recordings of people talking, they seldom transfer directly to the printed page. Therefore, I have edited all of the interviews for clarity and brevity and in some cases have rearranged the material slightly to make it flow more smoothly. As careful as I have been to check and recheck my sources, errors inevitably creep in, and I take responsibility for them.

Several years ago, Marsha Lotstein retired as executive director of the Jewish Historical Society and moved to Florida. However, she still allows

# Preface

me to call upon her for help. As in the past, Marsha has guided me, pointed out both the good and the bad in my manuscripts and has edited ruthlessly. I hope we will continue to work together on many more projects. Finally, I would like to thank my family, particularly my husband Herbert Hoffman, who struggles along with me during the process of putting a book together. Someday he will have real dinners and clean laundry again.

# Introduction

# Early Settlement

When the Reverend Thomas Hooker and a group of Congregationalists from Cambridge, Massachusetts founded Hartford, Connecticut in 1636, they claimed the land from the Connecticut River west for six miles. In 1675, a group of 97 proprietors divided 5,154 acres of Hartford's western wilderness into 7 long lots that became the basis for a new settlement in the West Division. It was not until 1713—thirty-five years after Thomas Hosmer and his son Stephen built a dam and sawmill on Trout Brook and established the center of the new community—that the Congregational Church permitted the western settlers to organize the Fourth Church of Hartford in the West Division.[1]

For nearly two centuries, the tight religious and political control of the Congregational Church did not allow for the development of other types of religious communities in Connecticut. Only with the disestablishment of the Congregational Church in 1818 were other Christian groups permitted to form their own congregations.

Although individual Jews lived in Hartford from its earliest years, little is known about them. David, the first Jew recorded in the public records, was cited for illegal trading in 1659, and the Vital Records of Hartford Land Distribution noted in 1667 that Jacob the Jew was a horse dealer. The name Jew Street appeared in newspaper advertisements in the late eighteenth century, but disappeared from use soon after. While other Jews were occasionally mentioned, they appeared to be transients and did not form a community.[2]

The first permanent group of Jews to make their homes in Hartford came from Germany as part of a larger wave of German immigration in the mid-nineteenth century. By the 1840s, approximately two hundred Jews were established in Hartford's immigrant East Side where they opened

# Introduction

*Left:* Touro Hall was the home of Congregation Beth Israel from 1856 to 1876.

*Opposite:* Congregation Beth Israel conducted services on Charter Oak Avenue in Hartford from 1876 to 1935.

small businesses or engaged in occupations, some of which reached beyond the immigrant community. Among them were horse dealers, clerks, Hebrew teachers, manufacturers and merchants.

It was not until 1843, when the Connecticut legislature amended the statutes to permit Jews the same rights as Christians, that Jews were allowed to form the first synagogue in Hartford. Congregation Beth Israel would also be the first synagogue to move to West Hartford nearly a century later.

During its early years, Beth Israel hired religious leaders, moved from members' homes to rented space, and in 1856 purchased the First Baptist Church building, renaming it Touro Hall. Following a fire that destroyed Touro Hall, they constructed the first synagogue building in Connecticut specifically for that purpose. By the time of the dedication of the new building in 1876, Beth Israel had also shifted from the Orthodox religious practices of Europe to the American Reform, allowing men and women to sit together during services, employing an organ and instituting Confirmation, a group ceremony designed to replace the individual Bar Mitzvah. These changes generated dissention among the congregants, some of whom broke away to form the Orthodox congregation Adas Yisroule in 1865. Twelve years later, however, that group disbanded, with most of the members returning to Beth Israel.

Meanwhile, members of Beth Israel founded men's and women's religious and social groups—primarily the Ararat Lodge of the national B'nai B'rith

# Early Settlement

association for men and the local Deborah Society for women. These served as the basis for the emerging social structure of the community. Overall, the immigrants were becoming Americans as symbolized by the transition from the German language to English in the synagogue and other organizations. As their economic status improved, many German Jews moved from the multi-ethnic East Side to the more prosperous neighborhoods to the south, near Beth Israel on Charter Oak Avenue, and to the West End, bordering West Hartford. By 1880, Hartford's German Jewish community numbered about 1,500 and was accepted as part of the multifaceted immigrant world of the growing city.

## THE WEST DIVISION

During this period, the West Division of Hartford was expanding and prospering. The 1790 census recorded a remarkably homogeneous population of approximately a thousand, with only a few African Americans—some slave, some free—in the community. Although the early settlers had primarily been farmers or worked in occupations that supported rural life, the situation was beginning to change.

In 1792, the long struggle to separate from Hartford began. Although a number of prominent residents opposed partition, other West Division

# Introduction

West Hartford Center, circa 1900. *Photograph courtesy of the Noah Webster House & West Hartford Historical Society.*

According to the 1860 census, immigrants like this group of brickyard workers in 1927 were primarily from Ireland, Sweden, France and Germany and were generally Lutheran or Roman Catholic. They worked in the potteries and other emerging industries of the south end of West Hartford, Elmwood. There is no record of Jews moving into the area at that time. *Photograph courtesy of the Noah Webster House & West Hartford Historical Society.*

# Early Settlement

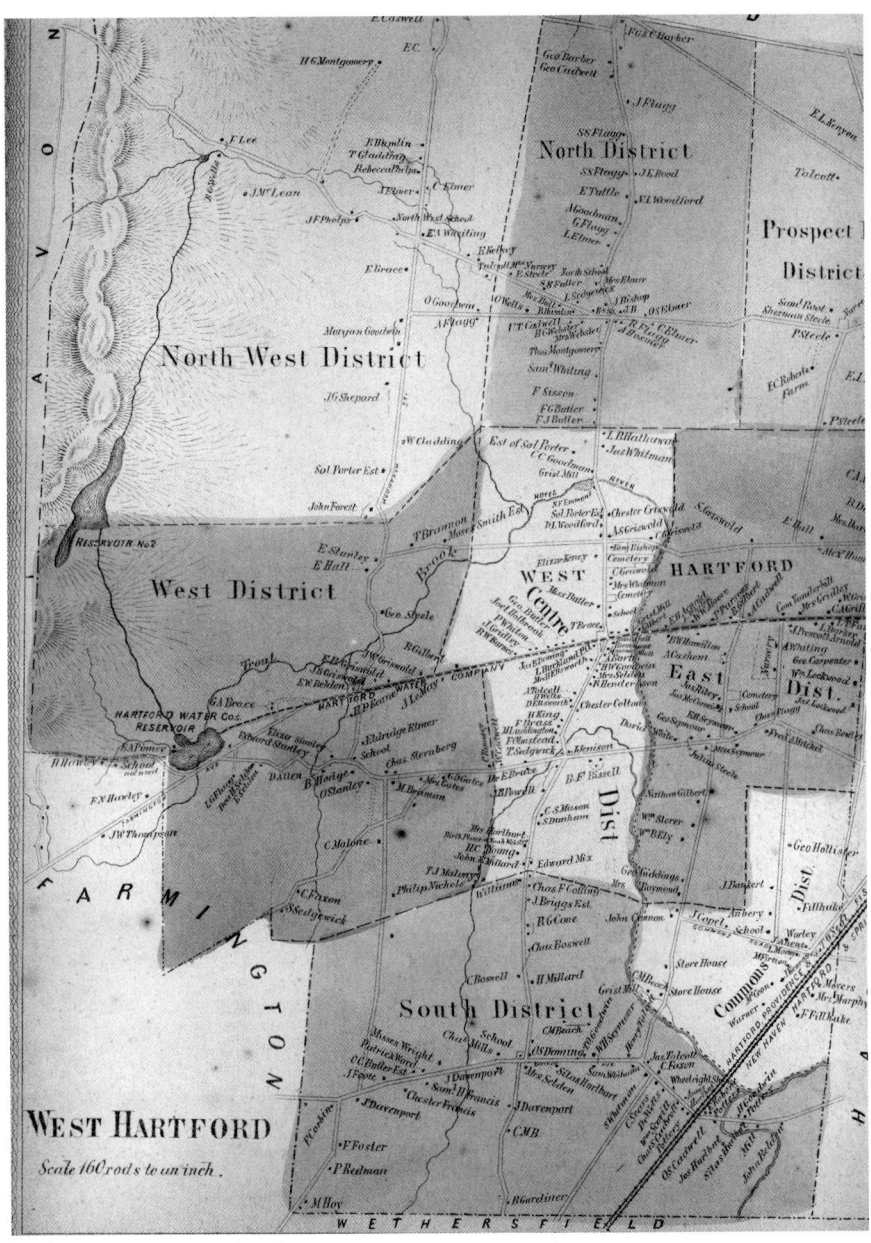

Baker & Tilden, Atlas of Hartford City and County, 1869.

leaders who were at odds with the Hartford political leadership wanted to control the affairs in their own community. In addition, the increasing national debate over slavery, states rights, education and, by mid-century, the rise of the new Republican Party deepened the divide between Hartford and its West Division. In 1854 the Connecticut General Assembly permitted West Hartford to become an independent community.[3]

## The Immigrants

In 1881, events in the Russian Empire precipitated what would become one of the largest Jewish emigrations from Eastern Europe and would completely change the face of Jewish life in the United States, including in Hartford. On March 1, Tsar Alexander II was assassinated by a revolutionary group that numbered only a few Jewish members. Nevertheless, the Jews became the focus of both government and mob retaliation and were the victims of a combination of discriminatory laws and *pogroms* (anti-Semitic violence and murder) that would continue for more than forty years. Millions of Jews left their homes, believing that life had to be better anywhere else. For many, the United States promised to be *die goldine medine*, the Golden Land.

Of the 6,500 Jews living in Hartford in 1910, only 20 percent were German Jewish, with the remainder coming from Eastern Europe and Russia.[4] Emma Cohen, who was born in Hartford and grew up on Governor Street in a Yiddish-speaking household, was well aware of the differences between the established German Jews and the Eastern European newcomers. She said,

> *For quite a while the German Jews acted as if they were superior. They were already Americanized, and here were the Russian Jews with these awful manners. Our ways were completely different, and we were probably much more active in all kinds of things. Because there were* [very few German Jews] *what happened was that we overcame them in numbers.*

Although money was scarce in many families and children often went to work, most Jews saw education as the critical step toward Americanization and tried to keep the children, including the girls, in school as long as possible. With the newcomers putting their trust in the Hartford schools to educate their children without discriminating against them because of their religion, the trend in religious education was toward supplemental after-school programs.

Morris Handler was born in Hartford in 1913 and lived most of his early years in the downtown immigrant neighborhood. When he was very

# Early Settlement

In the downtown area of Windsor, State and Front Streets near the Connecticut River, the Jewish newcomers thrived among the pushcarts, polyglot population and people determined to become good Americans. Immigrants opened businesses with as little capital as a horse and wagon, went to work in established firms, or created niches for themselves by adapting their European skills for the American market.

Emma Cohen (fifth from the right in the back row) was a member of the large Russian Jewish Sherry (originally Sheresherky) family shown in this 1914 photo. Victor Harris (third child from the left in the front row) is the grandfather of State Senator Jonathan Harris.

# Introduction

In 1934, the students of the Nelson Street Talmud Torah posed for their picture. (Seated left to right) Bernard Wilkins, Edith (Kriwitsky) Gittleman, Abraham Goldfarb, Joyce (Hershokowitz) Hershman, Harold Paskowitz. (Standing) Merril Rome, Harold Goldfarb, teacher Mr. Aaron Kriwitsky, William Slitt, Israel Tabatsky and Irving Luckman.

young, the family lived on Windsor Avenue in a Civil War arsenal that had been converted into apartments, but later moved to Market Street, where his parents opened a Russian steam bath and operated the *mikveh* (Jewish ritual bath). Although he attended public school during the day, Moe was expected to master Hebrew and religious subjects in the afternoon.

> *In Hebrew school we learned to read the letters which are the same for Yiddish. There were a lot of papers around so I picked up reading Yiddish too. We had in Hartford two public Hebrew schools. There was also a smaller private one. The Talmud Torah, where I went, was on Pleasant Street. It was a beautiful building that had a hall where they had weddings and other affairs. We had to climb two flights of stairs to the classroom, and we had another meeting room. Down in the basement, they had rooms for organizations that would come for meetings.*

Uncomfortable with the increasingly Reform Beth Israel, the Eastern Europeans formed prayer groups and synagogues based on the particular customs of their communities of origin. Founded between 1881 and the turn of the century were Adas Israel (1884); Agudas Achim, also know as the Romanian Hebrew Congregation (1887); Congregation Israel-Ateras Israel (1895); Shaarey Torah (1897) and Congregation Israel of Koretz, Anshe Koretz (1898). Over time additional Orthodox synagogues were founded, faltered, merged and moved. The first Conservative congregation, the Emanuel Synagogue, originally called B'nai Israel, opened in 1919.

Coming from a tradition of caring for those in need, members of the Jewish community collected funds to provide for the elderly, the ill, the unemployed, orphans and transients needing kosher meals and a cheap place to sleep. They also sent money abroad to those who were suffering from wars, anti-Semitism and general poverty. These early organizations—often combined and reconstructed over time—became the basis for the communal institutions that continue to serve the Jewish community. Among them were the Hebrew Ladies Sick Benefit Aid Association which formed a "Handkerchief Brigade" in 1907 to collect money to buy a house for the Hebrew Ladies Old People's Home, the precursor of the Hebrew Home and Hospital.

Beginning in the late 1870s, various groups organized recreational and educational programs for young people. Primary among these during the early years were the Young Men's Hebrew Association (YMHA) and later the Young Women's Hebrew Association (YWHA). In 1942, the Jewish Center Association took over the functions of its predecessors.

In response to the confusing number of small charities collecting for causes in Hartford and abroad, a mixed group of German and Eastern European immigrants formed the United Jewish Charities in 1912 to consolidate charitable giving and to provide financial assistance to Jewish families in need. This agency would later reorganize as the Jewish Family Service and in 1945 would relinquish its coordinating functions to the newly formed Hartford Jewish Federation, which would become the central clearinghouse for Hartford Jewish charities and services.

In 1923, Jewish doctors, citing the need for a hospital where they could practice without prejudice and where Jewish patients would receive kosher food and appropriate care, opened Mount Sinai Hospital on Capitol Avenue. Although Mount Sinai soon outgrew its building and its patient base was in the process of relocating to the North End, it was not able to move to Blue Hills Avenue until after World War II when it took over the former Children's Home and opened a 115 bed facility in 1950. During the following two decades, Mt. Sinai underwent several expansion and renovation projects, which increased the number of patient beds and provided intensive care units.

The cultural scene was dominated by groups of all sorts—political clubs, religious organizations, burial societies, charities, *landsmanschaften*

# Introduction

(organizations composed of those from the same cities or towns in Europe), *oxys* (free loan associations), music, theater and purely social clubs. The immigrants mixed with those from other countries in these organizations, forging a community that would continue to develop in Hartford until after World War II.

Between 1881 and 1920, international Jewish demographics changed radically, with more than a quarter of the estimated fifteen million Jews worldwide leaving their homes in the Russian Empire and other Eastern European countries. The majority, approximately 3.6 million, immigrated to the United States, with others going to Western Europe, South Africa, Palestine and South America. By the mid-1920s, the combination of the new Soviet Union's closing its doors to emigration and the institution of restrictive laws in the U.S. brought immigration nearly to a standstill, a condition that prevailed for decades. Southern and Eastern Europeans—many of whom were Catholic—and Jews suffered disproportionately under the stringent laws which provided larger quotas for those coming from more favored nations. Immigration in Hartford decreased accordingly, with the Jewish population settling at about eighteen thousand, approximately 10 percent of Hartford's total population.[5]

With immigration no longer an option, many of those who had been concerned with bringing their families from abroad and then absorbing them into Hartford's Jewish world turned their attention to community building. Throughout the 1920s and 1930s, the majority of the Jews flowed from the area of first settlement toward the northwestern part of the city. Morris Handler, who graduated from Hartford Public High in the class of 1931B, observed the changes that were taking place in the Jewish community.

> *Agudas Achim built* [a new synagogue] *in the 1920s to follow their people. That was on Greenfield Street. That was the general movement. The Garden Street area became the business center, and Garden Street and Enfield and all that was the North End. My father owned real estate there in the twenties. A lot of us stayed on this side of the park. Keney Park was where I met my wife, by the way. That's where all the young people in my time met. Keney Park was the center.*
>
> *Then on the other side of the park, a lot of building was going on. After World War I, building really started up. The North End was where a lot of painters and sheet-metal men, and carpenters, tradespeople were living, the ones who helped the building, the Jewish ones. They had some Italians in the neighborhood, and they were the bricklayers and the masons. The Jewish kids dominated* [at Weaver, the local high school opposite

# Early Settlement

> Keney Park]: *salutatorian, valedictorian, and there were the football players and the basketball players too. They were into everything.* [The Jews] *had a marvelous reputation. Kids went to any college they wanted to if they had the stuff. No prep school enjoyed a better reputation.*

Not all Jews, however, lived in the North End. Some, like Calvin Mass's father, who arrived in Hartford about 1910, settled in more remote neighborhoods to be near their businesses. Calvin, the youngest of their four children and the only one born in America, remembers growing up in Hartford.

> *I started in the South End because my father, who was a tailor, had a shop on Park Street. There were several Jewish families in the South End. Most of the Jews in the early years were either in the northeast or northwest part of Hartford. The northeast was sort of the blue-collar section, and the northwest was the people that had more money or they were here a generation. Actually, I lived off of Park Street on Ashton Street, which is off of Heath Street. I only lived there until I was about seven years old, and then because* [of] *my sister Betty, who was at time just before her pre-teens—my mother was afraid she would go around with* [non-Jewish boys]*—we moved up to the North End, up to Earle Street on the northeast section of Hartford.*
>
> *Park Street and my family are really connected because my father had a business on Park Street. My brother Sidney practiced* [as a dentist] *on Park Street. My brother Sam had a business on Park Street, a fruit business for a while, and my son, Martin Mass, is an optometrist, who is still on Park Street. Park Street, even though I was brought up in the North End is really integral in my family.*

Although the community continued to flourish, individuals were already beginning to move toward the suburbs, particularly West Hartford and, to a lesser extent, Bloomfield. A few trickled out in the 1930s, with the number increasing every decade, until only a few isolated families remain today. Over time, the Jewish merchants, synagogues and communal institutions followed their constituents. When the Hebrew Home moved to its new facility in West Hartford in 1989, only Mount Sinai Hospital remained, and it was soon to be absorbed by Saint Francis Hospital and to lose its Jewish identification completely.

## Chapter One

# Moving West

At the turn of the twentieth century, West Hartford—with a population of 3,186, compared to Hartford's 79,850—was just beginning its transformation from sleepy rural community to the multi-faceted town it would become by the middle of the century. The crossroads at North Main Street and the Albany Turnpike, two miles north of the Center, which would become the primary Jewish neighborhood after 1950, had been an established stagecoach stop and business center surrounded by the farms of the West Division for more than a hundred years. The intersection took its name from the tobacco farm and warehouse opened by Joseph Bishop in 1842. Nearby were Eliza Mansfield's strawberry farm; Frank Strong's blacksmith, wheelwright, and wagon shop and the North School.

While industrial workers and other laborers, many them foreign-born, settled in the southeastern section of town in the early years of the century, by the 1920s, other families, slightly higher on the socio-economic ladder, filled the apartments in the two- and three-family frame houses and small apartment buildings that characterized the side streets near the intersection of Farmington Avenue and South Quaker Lane. The most affluent bought big houses in the newly developing areas near Elizabeth Park and the planned communities of West Hill, Sunny Reach, Sunset Farm and Woodridge Lake. Even so, large areas of town were still open farmland, particularly in the north near Bishops Corner. The census reflected the rapid growth of the town during this period: 1910: 4,898, 1920: 8,894, 1930: 24,941 and 1940: 33,776.[6]

By the mid-1930s, some Jewish families were beginning to leave the area of second settlement, the North End. Some wanted to escape the tight Jewish atmosphere of the city, while others looked only at real estate values.

# Jewish West Hartford

Workers stand outside Frank Strong's blacksmith, wagon and wheel shop near the intersection of Flagg Road and North Main Street in Bishops Corner. (Left to right) Herb Messenger, owner Herb Strong, Louis Chaffee, Hiho Ward, Heman Hamlin, unknown, William Nichols and Edw. Nichols. *Photo courtesy of the Noah Webster House & West Hartford Historical Society.*

In some cases, individuals opened branches of their Hartford businesses in West Hartford or in the surrounding suburbs. Others transferred their entire operations to the suburbs, and still others created new businesses. A few moved back and forth between Hartford and West Hartford as their finances and family needs changed.

Later, after World War II, as part of a national trend toward mixing with members of other white ethnic groups, young second- and third-generation Americans—Jews among them—who had attended public schools, spoke unaccented English, and had served in the armed forces were looking beyond their former inner-city neighborhoods. Many used their government benefits for higher education, which would increase their earning potential and allow them to buy new homes in the suburbs. As Moe Handler, who moved to West Hartford in 1950, put it, "There was a big transition into the single family syndrome, and more of us could afford houses."

Among the earliest families to move to West Hartford was that of Frances Schwartz Feldman, whose father had a business on the West Hartford end of Park Street, Park Road.

# Moving West

*I was born in 1924, and I became ill. I had pneumonia, and the doctor said to my parents, "You have to go west." So we went into West Hartford. I was maybe two years old. We moved to Park Road and Quaker Lane. Several blocks down there was a Park Road Department Store, which was owned by* [a Jewish family], *and then there was another family in the roofing business, but basically where I lived we were the only Jewish people.*

*My father had opened up a grocery store—not kosher at all—in a completely gentile neighborhood. We had no anti-Semitic feeling at all shown.* [The customers] *were from all around, way up west like Ridgewood Road. We had Swedish customers.* [My father] *had a truck. He delivered groceries to all of his customers who needed deliveries, who couldn't get out, who didn't have cars.* [My mother worked in the business, but] *I was young at that time. I was still going to school.*

*I went to Seymour Avenue, Florence Smith School. I went to Alfred Plant Junior High on Whiting Lane, and then I went to the old Hall. I graduated from there and went off to Boston University in Boston. Nobody cared* [in the elementary school that we were Jewish]. *It was a good way of life. At Hall High, I would say a very small percentage, less than one percent, were Jewish. They lived north of Farmington Avenue. Some lived on Auburn Road. Some lived off of South Quaker Lane. Many people who lived in that area went to Beth Israel, the reformed synagogue. For my education I went to Beth Israel only because I had to walk. I had no means of transportation because my parents were so busy. I was confirmed; they didn't have the Bar Mitzvah.*

*What did kids do* [in the 1930s in West Hartford]? *They played marbles. They just entertained themselves. They would build little radios, just the boys. I had to* [help with housework] *because my folks worked all day long and came up late at night. My mother did the washing late at night.* [I was expected to] *behave myself and study. Education, that's all they stressed.*

After graduating from Boston University as a physical therapist, Fran took a job in Newington and moved back in with her parents. She had lost touch with her high school friends.

*My parents moved to Farmington Avenue about eight streets west of West Hartford Center, and I joined the YPL at the Emanuel Synagogue in Hartford, the Young People's League. I met a lot of my high school friends, and then all the folks who came back from the service. Then I*

# Jewish West Hartford

The old Hall High School is now the West Hartford Town Hall. *Photograph courtesy of the Noah Webster House & West Hartford Historical Society.*

*joined Junior Hadassah. We had our meetings, and we taught songs to the Young Judeans* [a Hadassah children's group]. *I met my husband at the Young People's League. I was with Hadassah, and I was selling tickets for a dance. I said, "Would you buy a ticket for this dance? You know it's for a good cause." And he said very facetiously, "I will buy a ticket if you will go with me." And I did.*

*We stayed in West Hartford just for two years* [after the wedding], *and then we got a small house on Tower Avenue in Hartford, and we lived there until our daughter was a junior at Weaver. We moved to West Hartford in the early sixties because the house was too small. We had four children. We found this house on West Ridge Road. This is the only house we've been in ever since. The new Hall High is two blocks away. It's just a perfect situation.*

*After the war, people were looking for places. They moved to West Hartford. They moved to Bloomfield. When we bought, I didn't even think about* [the possibility of not being welcome in other parts of West Hartford although we knew about] *upper Ridgewood Road, Wood Pond. We just came here because we had all Jewish neighbors. This was so convenient because we were right near Beth El. A friend of mine still lives in Hartford, and she will never move. She loves it. She has a good*

# Moving West

The Young People's League of the Emanuel Synagogue put on one of its annual shows on May 16, 1954.

*relationship with her neighbors. Well, it's kind of hard there. I mean all of a sudden, this very vibrant Jewish community broke up and moved to the suburbs, and they were replaced by different ethnic groups.*

Although the Jewish community in Hartford was still primarily centered in Hartford's North End, by the 1930s, additional families had begun to follow the trail to the suburbs. Martin Epstein's parents were some of the first Jews in 1933 to buy in their neighborhood on Griswold Drive near Asylum Avenue. Although Marty's oldest friend in the neighborhood was Jewish, as a young child, he was not particularly aware of the other Jews in the predominately Christian area. He attended Morley School, Plant Junior High and the old Hall High School in West Hartford Center.

[Before I was born, my parents] *were living in the famous North End of Harford on Elmer Street, I think in a house owned by my father's parents, so things were a little tight. This was during the Depression. My father had a job, which was unusual, and they had saved some money and could buy a house and a lot for $5,000. He was working in the post office at that time.*

*I had an aunt and uncle and two cousins that lived on Park Road in West Hartford. That was like getting out of the ghetto and going into the Christian world. My cousin went to the Smith School. I think there was maybe one other Jewish kid in the school. My uncle had an upholstery shop on Park Road. They owned an apartment house, and they had an apartment there.*

[In the 1940s] *we did Christmas* [at Morley School]. *Nowadays, a Jewish family would rebel at having their kids participate in a Christmas pageant, but in those days we did, and as I look back, it is kind of surprising to me that there weren't objections, but maybe there were objections or maybe my parents were intimidated or just thought maybe that's just the way it is here.*

*Some of my Jewish friends went to private school so just a few went to Plant. In junior high one of my friends was named Johnson, and what kind of struck me was that for him and his friends whether you were Jewish or not didn't register at all. They made no distinction, and I thought they were a little bit more accepting of others than we Jews were. So you had quite a lot of Jews by the time I got to high school and certainly a lot of Swedes.* [My friends were] *mostly the Jewish kids. I don't think that our activities were any different. You even had Jewish kids on the football team. It wasn't unusual for those days.*

*I went to the* [West Hartford] *Jewish Center, the precursor of Beth David* [Synagogue] *to Hebrew School, and I think I was part of the first class. It was the first Orthodox synagogue in West Hartford, and there were a lot of Jews looking for something like that because they wanted to go to synagogue in West Hartford.*

*Later, when I got of law school, I moved in with my parents* [on Griswold] *for a year or two, and then I got an apartment in Hartford. After that I went to Israel for two years, and I got married in 1971 when we were there.* [Then we came back to West Hartford] *to Oakwood Avenue, back in the South End. When we felt it would be a good time to buy a house, we came down this street, and there was a man across the street who said, "This is a great house. You buy this house." This was '74. I think Mohawk Drive* [was always a Jewish neighborhood]. *It was known as the Jewish "reservation"* [because of the Native American names of the streets]. *I believe it was built in 1954. We were right near King Phillip School and not too far from* [the new] *Hall High. You can say "I'm not going to move to the reservation because it's too stereotypical," but when push comes to shove, these things do become important.*

Nan Lewis Glass, who served as Mayor from 1995-1997, remembers the early days of the Jewish migration to West Hartford.

## Moving West

With Grandmother Anna Epstein keeping a watchful eye from the doorway, cousins Reed Margolis, Cynthia Dortz and Martin Epstein played in the Epsteins' front yard. *Photograph courtesy of Martin Epstein.*

# Jewish West Hartford

"As you came in from Asylum Avenue, I think my parents' house was the last one. A good part of Griswold Drive between Fern and Asylum was still woods. If you bought a lot on Griswold Drive, there was a lottery, and one of the purchasers had a chance to win a house on the corner of Griswold and Bainbridge." —Martin Epstein *Photograph courtesy of Martin Epstein.*

*There was a huge explosion of Jewish immigration into West Hartford after the Second World War with the building of the "reservation" and what have you, but there were Jews in West Hartford before that. We moved to West Hartford before I was eleven years old. I went to Alfred Plant Junior High School and Hall High School. I graduated in 1946.*

*We lived on Milton Street. My father worked at the* Hartford Times, *and he and two other gentleman at the time brought three blocks of an undeveloped area off Robin Road. I think we were there a little bit before Beth David, but my parents were members of Emanuel Synagogue. When we moved there, it was A.C. Peterson's dairy farm. There was just a grazing area between Robin Road down to the brook. When I went to high school, I walked down the dirt path to get to Farmington Avenue. Trout Brook Drive was not completed through to Farmington Avenue until after World War II.*

*Some of my Jewish classmates ended up going Kingswood or Oxford, but there were a lot of Jewish kids in my Hall High class of '46. I had non-Jewish friends at high school but socialized with the Jewish kids on the weekends or dating or anything like that. Most of the Jewish kids were from Weaver. There was some hierarchal stuff going on because many of the Jews who were in West Hartford before we came in the forties were*

# Moving West

Nan Glass and her date—Stanley Solomkin, a navy Seabee—attended her junior prom at Hall High in 1945. *Photograph courtesy of Nan Glass.*

*the German Jews. But as far as direct prejudice or antagonism, no, I can't say that.*

*Then I went to UConn [the University of Connecticut]. I had the luxury of being an English major and a political science minor. Those two things have followed me all my life, my career. I graduated from UConn in 1950, went back and worked there for a year in the Public Information Office. I got married in 1951, and my then husband was getting his PhD, so for the next five years or so I lived in the Pennsylvania/New Jersey area, and then we came back to this area, lived in Tariffville which is out in Simsbury. One of the reasons we moved back to West Hartford—I liked Tariffville—was my children started to go to Hebrew school, and I was driving them to West Hartford three times a week, and it got ridiculous after a while. But Hartford, West Hartford is always the center of our family life. Most of the family was in West Hartford by the fifties and sixties.*

When Stanley Weisen's father opened a branch of his Hartford sporting goods store in West Hartford Center in the mid-1930s, the family soon followed, making their home in the new neighborhood between Fern and Asylum Streets. Throughout his more than fifty-year career selling glass products to builders, Stanley dealt with many of those who developed West Hartford.[7]

*In 1936 we moved to Foxcroft Road. There were four bedrooms, a bigger house and a big yard. I graduated from Hall High School in 1938. At that time there were eight Jewish children in the class out of three hundred and twenty. We played basketball. "Here come the guys who eat no ham." There were comments like that, but there was no prejudice then. I was on the basketball team and on the track team. It helped me [to make friends easily]. One Jewish fellow in the class and I were very good dancers. So when we went to the different dances, the women, the kids, used to like to dance with us, the jitterbug and all that. In between sports I worked in the Sport Center, on Farmington Avenue. I used to help my father. [When I was] twelve, thirteen, fourteen, I would go downtown and dress windows. I would sweep the floor, and I learned how to string tennis rackets.*

*I went in the Army January 15, 1942. My folks had moved to Bloomfield, so we lived there for a little while [after the war. When I got married, we lived] on Bloomfield Avenue with my in-laws, and then we moved to Robin Road. I worked for my father after I got out of the service until 1951, and then I went to work for my brother-in-law and father-in-law in the glass business.*

# Moving West

*A lot of these Jewish builders started building apartment houses in Hartford. Bernie and Eddie Waldman built a lot of houses, not necessarily for Jewish people but all over the area. These builders like Bernie and [Bernard and Joseph] Friedman, they would buy the whole tract of land. The Friedmans built all those houses across the street from the Jewish Community Center [off Bloomfield Avenue]. I would say 75 percent of those people were Jewish. They built Hampshire House. They were building all these apartment houses in Hartford, and then they moved to West Hartford. Leo Reiner built the apartment houses on Farmington Avenue. Almost all the apartment houses were built by Jewish builders. [Jews moved into these] three-bedroom, two-bedroom apartment houses for a while and then moved to houses.*

*There was a lot of empty space, land in West Hartford off of Albany Avenue, off of Asylum Avenue, and that's where the builders started building. One of the first real big builders was Irving Stitch. There were different builders on different streets. Richard Schlomberg started building on Whitehill, and then there came Jerry Kelter. A lot of builders would buy six or eight tracts. One of the biggest builders were the McGalty Brothers [who were not Jewish]. They built tons of houses here on Craigmoor and on different streets.*

*And then north, like on Mountain Road, Mike Baldwin built the first houses, and then Bernie Lapuk built the rest of those houses off of Mountain Road going out. On Seminole Circle, all those houses were built by Neil Ellis, Green Manors. That was a construction company. And then further down that was Stone and Goldberg. They built the houses on the other side of the synagogue, but the biggest builder across from Emanuel was Jerry Kelter, built maybe a hundred and fifty houses, something like that. Then up on the Mountain came custom building, like Irving Stitch built his house which was a big one, one of the first ones up there. And then mostly Jewish people [were buying the houses in the north end at that point]. I would say the bulk of them.*

When Calvin Mass was released from the Army in 1946, he returned to West Hartford with his wife Helen and baby son, Marty. Their first apartment was on Loomis Drive, and their second, after their daughter Nan was born, on Arnold Way where they lived until they bought a house in the heart of the Jewish reservation, a short distance from Bishops Corner.

*We moved here in 1950, to Osage Road, West Hartford. We looked at the plans. Paul Uremko and Brothers were very good builders. I wanted a ranch house. He built six ranch houses on the left side of the street and six colonials*

> on the right side, and at the end of the street was a farm, Farmer Brown, with cows in 1950. And on my property, believe it or not, was a windmill up on the hill, about a hundred and fifty feet from the house. I think it was pumping water from a well. It was just off of North Main Street, which wasn't developed. It was wonderful for us. Our kids grew up here sort of in a bucolic atmosphere. They used to climb the trees. The street was full of kids.
>
> We are the only original remaining family on Osage Road. Osage Road ended at Farmer Brown's property. During the seventies somebody bought Farmer Brown's property and made a cul-de-sac, and they built seven to eight houses. So it's the same quiet street it was, practically, when we came here. It was always a mixed street, but I think it has a few more non-Jews now. On this side of the street, a family from Sri Lanka moved in. They are gunsmiths, very talented people that work on ancient gunstocks and restore them. They are very good neighbors, wonderful neighbors. The street has become cosmopolitan.

By the early 1950s, the transformation of the farmland around Bishops Corner into small plots with hundreds of single-family homes had begun. Commercial developers responded by providing additional stores and services in the Corner. The most notable new buildings were the Allstate Insurance Company regional office—the largest office employer in town—and the Lord & Taylor department store. The latter had been the subject of an intense battle between William A. Mauser, the developer, and the Town Council on one side and the West Hartford Home Owners' Association and Beatrice F. Auerbach of the downtown G. Fox Hartford department store family on the other. Despite the elegance of the first branch of the New York store in Connecticut, gas stations and parking lots have characterized the Corner since 1931 when Katherine and David Welch, owners of Welch's Inn, a popular restaurant in the 1920s, sold their corner property to Standard Oil.[8] Said Helen Mass,

> On the northwest corner was Dutchland Farms. We went there for ice cream. There was a country store with everything, vegetables and fruit. You picked what you wanted, got a slip, and went to someone else to pay for it and then back to pick it up. There wasn't much on the northeast corner. Then they built that up. It made it easier for us. We used to walk to the Corner. We had the hill, which kind of killed us at the time, but we used to push the baby carriage up it. Bishops Corner changed considerably. The big change was when Lord & Taylor came here and built that building on the southwest corner [on the site of Dutchland Farms].

# Moving West

Dutchland Farms in Bishops Corner. *Photograph courtesy of the Noah Webster House & West Hartford Historical Society.*

Lord & Taylor in Bishops Corner. *Photograph courtesy of the Noah Webster House & West Hartford Historical Society.*

# Jewish West Hartford

While Calvin and Helen Mass had made a conscious decision to make their home in a primarily Jewish neighborhood, New Yorker Marsha Lotstein, who came to West Hartford toward the end of the building boom in 1969, was not aware of the distinct divisions between neighborhoods populated by different ethnic or religious groups.

*We lived in East Hartford for two years, and then we moved to West Hartford. We first moved to a house in what is known as Astronaut Village, right down on New Britain Avenue, opposite Westfarms Mall. At the time there was no Westfarms Mall. It was all woods. There was a golf driving range. It was very nice: colonials, raised ranches and split-level homes. We liked the house, and we had some neighbors from East Hartford that were moving there, so we bought this place.*

*To me, West Hartford was West Hartford. I later came to find out that we were one of probably five Jewish families in this whole development. I had nobody to carpool to Hebrew school with. I found it very hard to make friends because they didn't share the same interests. My daughter was the only Jewish kid in her class at Wolcott School. Whenever there was a big Jewish holiday, I brought food in. I always had Chanukah parties. I always had to work harder at being Jewish while in New York you don't have to work at it.*

*My next-door neighbor was a Catholic family. We became very, very close. We shared a lot of things, and we helped each other out all the time. We were in the cul-de-sac, and there were five houses. Another of the houses had four children, and the youngest daughter was about a year older than my daughter. One time my daughter was complaining there was nobody to play with, and I said, "Go outside. Go play with Susie." And she said, "I can't." I said, "What do you mean, you can't?" "Well, she told me she can't play with me because I'm Jewish." My daughter was five, and this kid was six.*

*When I heard about a petition being organized to make a black professional couple move out of the neighborhood, I said to my husband, "That's it." That was the straw that broke the camel's back! "If they're saying that about these very nice people, God knows what they're saying about us. We're getting out of here." I was determined to come to an area, a neighborhood where I would feel comfortable, where I felt my children would be respected and they had friends. [The Lotsteins moved to Porter Drive near Asylum Avenue.]* [9]

Over the years, the incidences of anti-Semitism in West Hartford have been relatively mild. Undoubtedly, individuals who were not pleased with

Seth and Debbie Lotstein play in the front yard of their house in Astronaut Village. *Photograph courtesy of Marsha Lotstein.*

the large percentage of Jews in town made comments to Jewish neighbors or grumbled more generally about the town not being what it used to be. Although statements of this sort are painful for Jews, these opinions rarely translated into action. Even so, football games between archrivals Conard in the South End and Hall have been marred by partisan supporters shouting negative comments about Hall's Jewish players. Occasional swastikas and negative graffiti have appeared on buildings, and in 1977 two men were arrested for writing anti-Semitic slogans on cars and houses and starting several car fires. Public response has always been immediate and supportive of the Jews. Nothing that has happened in town has come close to the casually expressed prejudice that was tolerated in earlier years in America or which exists abroad.

More serious and with long-term implications were the mid-century real estate steering and restrictive covenants, which attempted to control residential patterns by discouraging Jews from buying in some neighborhoods. Even so, with many new houses available in new developments and in all price ranges, many Jews were not concerned about restricted neighborhoods, which they did not see as meeting their needs. Helen Mass remembers looking for a house in the late 1940s.

> *I think when we were going around looking at different places, at that time the real estate agent was gearing us away from many of the gentile neighborhoods. Frankly, I'd just as soon be with other Jews.*

Rabbi Stanley Kessler, then the new young rabbi of the fledgling Beth El Temple, fought the restrictive covenants, argued against religion in the public schools and generally worked to educate the majority population about issues of importance to Jews.

> *Some [Jews] wanted to move to [restricted areas] and came to me with those stories that were troubling to me. Two realtors in Greater Hartford, in particular, I had confrontations with. I felt [I was able to institute change] as a result of knowing who their clergy person was. [I let them know] something un-American was going on and would hurt the future of relationships between people. I expected that there would be changes. I felt [steering] was important to address.*
>
> *A lot of that changed because of the relationships with clergy people here. Early on, I was part of a small group that developed a clergy fellowship, and that fellowship became a very powerful force in West Hartford. Rabbi Abraham J. Feldman of Beth Israel had many years of establishing relationships with [the non-Jewish] clergy people. I had relationships with some of the younger clergymen. (There weren't any women at that time.)*
>
> *There were some really interesting issues like Bible reading in the public schools and having them realize what this meant in a larger picture where the New Testament was being read to a class where 98 percent were Jews. We had to deal with the Christmas issue in the public school. My sense is that much was done during those years, and a lot of my time went to addressing such issues.*

As late as the early 1970s, however, some steering was still taking place. Linda Hirsh, a *Hartford Courant* staff writer wrote about her personal experience with this practice.

# Moving West

> *A realtor helping my family find a home in West Hartford spread a map of the town on the floor. He proceeded to outline the Duffy School neighborhood with a Day-Glo green felt-tipped pen and adorned it with a crucifix. His hand crossed Farmington Avenue and found a section residents call the Reservation because the streets bear the names of Native American tribes. Within its borders, he drew a Star of David. "You would be more comfortable here," he said. After watching him mark several other areas with stars and crosses, we moved into one of the few sections where a cross and a star coexisted.*[10]

The fact that the Jews were not moving into established Yankee or heavily working-class European ethnic neighborhoods may have been one of the reasons why expressions of anti-Semitism were limited in West Hartford. Even though some of the new areas in the South End had been built by Jewish builders, few Jews bought houses there. Meanwhile the streets north and west of Bishops Corner continued to be magnets for Jewish families. As one Jewish old-timer put it, Jewish West Hartford consisted of an "upper ghetto" west of Mountain Road where the wealthy, many of them real estate developers, built large modern houses, and the "lower ghetto" near King Philip school where the young families congregated.

Real estate steering eventually succumbed to social pressure and new laws, and previously restricted neighborhoods opened to Jews and immigrants who come from countries that were completely outside of the experience of those living in West Hartford fifty years ago. The converse is also true with non-Jews of all backgrounds moving into formerly Jewish neighborhoods.

Among the newcomers settling in West Hartford during the latter part of the century were a number of Israelis. In a classic example of chain migration where one family brings another, Moshe and Dorit Elkayam and their children arrived in 1987. Although Moshe was eager for the move, Dorit was reluctant to leave her family. Said Moshe,

> *I always dreamed to come to the United States. My sister got married with American Jewish guy, and they moved to United States. It was a very hard time. We lived on Bretton Road about four years, and then we bought this house on Fuller Drive in 1991. My wife, she said, "That's it. That's what I want." Because we know that here it's a lot of Jewish people.*
>
> *[In Israel,] I was self-employed. I [learned welding] in school, and my father had the same business, so I used to work with my father. My first job [in America] was in a welding shop. Then I quit, and I work with one carpenter about one year and then go back to welding shop, but*

Dorit Elkayam and the children in her home daycare dress up for Halloween. *Photograph courtesy of Dorit Elkayman.*

*decided to work for myself, and that's how I start my business. I started as a handyman first—carpenter, remodeling, repair. I got a license for state of Connecticut for home improvement. Then I started to do plumbing, and somebody complain about me I don't have a license. I don't realize if I got one license, I need another one. I got some friend—he's Israeli, too—he took me to work. I learned the whole code plumbing in the United States, in Connecticut. Then I started the process to get my license. I took a couple courses, and then I took the exam. That's what I do now, plumbing—Mark's Plumbing—I think it's easier to say Mark than say Moshe for Americans.*

In the early days, Dorit depended upon her husband's family to help her shop for food with unfamiliar labels, pay bills and translate. Although she was a trained nursery-school teacher, Dorit knew that she would have to take any kind of a job, at least initially, to help support the family. Eventually, she built her own bilingual-daycare business at home.

*From the beginning, I couldn't get work because I didn't know English. I came here. I didn't know one word with three kids. So my brother-in-law used to have a bakery in [Crown] Supermarket, I used to work there.*

# Moving West

Dorit and Moshe Elkayam vacation in Prague.

*Communication was with the hand, with the eyes. I used to sell bread and slice challah. It was familiar for me because in Israel, challah is challah, cake is cake. In Israel, I worked for somebody else* [in a daycare center]. *It's not popular like here, small daycares. I start here with one child, two children. I start* [with babies] *from six weeks until three, four* [years old]. *It was extra successful the daycare. If I know before, I would buy a different house, special for daycare.*

Keen observers of the West Hartford scene, both Nan Glass and Marsha Lotstein have noted the population shift. Said Nan Glass:

*It seems to me that it was about ten years ago that I noticed the thing that really clued me in.* [I was] *driving around and seeing Christmas decorations in the North End of West Hartford, streets that were traditionally Jewish close to King Phillip School. That told me that West Hartford, that the neighborhoods were changing.*

Marsha Lotstein also tracked the change.

*The "reservation," as they call it, the King Philip area, when I first came was predominantly Jewish. And, you know, quote, the Jews were on one side, and everybody else was on the other side. But, it really isn't so. When I drive now—I've been driving for twenty years through King Philip and Mohegan Drives—I've noticed how the original owners, who bought those houses in the fifties, are selling now. Many are seniors and moving to other places or they're dying. For the most part, the newcomers are Indians from India or black people, Asian. There are also many more Orthodox Jews moving in because of the proximity to Chabad and Young Israel synagogues. So the whole demographics of this neighborhood, this area has changed. I'm sure it's the same where we used to live on the other side of town where it was heavily Italian.*[11]

Chapter Two

# The Pioneer Synagogues

## Congregation Beth Israel
### 701 Farmington Avenue

In 1920, Isidore Wise, the president of Beth Israel from 1907–1942, proposed that the congregation build a new building to accommodate its members who were moving to the fashionable West End or over the line to West Hartford. Wise—an owner of Wise, Smith & Company, a department store in Hartford, and a world traveler—had strong opinions about architecture. According to Marjorie L. Rafal:

> *It was when [the Wises] were in Istanbul that Mr. Wise became enamored of the ancient mosque of Hagia Sofia; he brought home copies of the drawings of the Byzantine mosque's design and these the architect used in the plans for the new Temple Beth Israel—for which all funds were raised before construction. There was no mortgage!*[12]

Rabbi Abraham J. Feldman, who had come to Beth Israel in 1925 as the congregation's twelfth rabbi, was equally concerned about the design.

> *We wanted this synagogue to be expressive in line and color of the religion which the synagogue was to represent and to teach. In the first place, in the selection of the site we remembered the ancient rabbinic thought that a synagogue ought to be on an elevated location and on a main thoroughfare...Our thought was that we Jews are a people deriving from the Orient, but also a people that has spent the greater part of its history in the Occident...If there were a type of architecture which represented the point of meeting of East and West, that architecture might express the idea we had. We found that such an architecture exists in the Byzantine type.*[13]

# The Hartford

44 PAGES HARTFORD, CONN. FRIDAY, DECEMBER 1, 1933

## Leading Figures in Beth Israel Cornerstone Laying

Left to right: Maurice Hartman, vice-president; Judge Elsner, treasurer, and Isidore Wise, president of Congregation Beth Israel; the Rev. William T. Hooper, rector of St. John's Episcopal church; the Rev. Dr. Robbins W. Barstow, president of the Hartford Seminary Foundation; Rbbi Morris Silverman of Emanuel synagogue; Frederick C. Opper, secretary of Beth Israel; Simon Kashmann, only living ex-president of Beth Israel; Rabbi Abraham J. Feldman of Beth Israel; Jacob Leipziger, president of the Southern New England Contracting company, and the Rev. Dr. John Newton Lackey, pastor of the Central Baptist church.

## TEMPLE CEREMONY LINKS GENERATIONS

Wise, Fox, Kashmann Saw Beth Israel's Cornerstone Laying in 1876—St. John's Church Greets Neighbor—Dr. Barstow and Rabbi Silverman Plead for Brotherhood.

Back in 1876, amid rejoicing and celebration, a congregation, Beth Israel, laid the cornerstone for a temple on Charter Oak avenue. Yesterday afternoon with the added import of a holiday of thanksgiving and in the presence of several hundred members and many Christian friends, a cornerstone was laid for the new temple of Beth Israel on Farmington avenue, near South Highland street, West Hartford.

Three Recall '76 Ceremony.

Among those who witnessed the [illegible] fifty-seven years ago, were [illegible] who participated in yesterday's [illegible] was Marx Fox, [illegible] living member of the congregation. Another was Simon Kashman, now 78 and the only living ex-president of the congregation. He was president when the Charter Oak avenue synagogue was enlarged, and his was the hand that destroyed the mortgage. Yesterday, this gray-haired old man, his face beaming joy, laid the records in the box that was placed within the corner stone. Among these effects was Rabbi Abraham J. Feldman's "Message to the Future," written on parchment. Maurice Hartman, vice-president, sealed the box.

A third witness of 1876 was Isidore Wise, who was only 11 years of age then. He has been president of Beth

## Temple Beth Israel To Lay Cornerstone

Exercises Will Be Held To-morrow at No. 701 Farmington Avenue.

With simple ceremonies, on a day of religious and patriotic meaning, the cornerstone of the new synagogue of Temple Beth Israel at No. 701 Farmington avenue, West Hartford, will be laid to-morrow, Thanksgiving day, at 3 o'clock. A large number of the congregation, friends, and representatives of churches and other synagogues will be present.

Of particular interest will be the ceremony of depositing records in a box, to be sealed in the cornerstone. This will be done by Simon Kashmann, only living ex-president of the congregation. Maurice Hartman, vice-president for twenty-seven years, will formally lay the cornerstone.

In the sealed box will be two copies of the Bible, one in English and one in Hebrew, a roster of the present members of the congregation, a roster of donors to the building fund and a roster of special gifts presented in honor of the cornerstone laying, all written in longhand by Frederick C. Opper on parchment. A copy of The Hartford Times of to-day and one of The Hartford Courant of to-morrow, a copy of the Jewish Ledger of November 24, wrapped in parchment and sealed, will be placed along with volumes of Rabbi Feldman's sermons "Hills to Climb" and "The Faith of

(CONTINUED ON PAGE 13)

# The Pioneer Synagogues

*Temple Beth Israel, Hartford, Conn.*

In 1936, Beth Israel moved from Charter Oak Avenue to Farmington Avenue in West Hartford. Not only was it the only Reform synagogue in the region, but it was the first synagogue of any sort to move to West Hartford.

During his forty-three years at Beth Israel, Rabbi Feldman was an active member of the community at large as well as of both the local and broader Jewish communities. Always concerned with inter-group relations, he was one of the founders of a cross-denominational rabbinical group, taught an introductory course on Judaism at the Hartford Seminary and was active in interfaith groups. In addition, he was an ardent Zionist, a stance that was not universally popular among Reform rabbis in the early years, and as a co-founder of the *Connecticut Jewish Ledger*, wrote strong editorials on that topic. At Beth Israel, Rabbi Feldman oversaw a number of changes in religious practice. Some of these eliminated customs, which "classic" American Reform perceived as unnecessary or archaic, while a number of other practices such as the reading of the *Megillah* [the Book of Esther] on Purim and blowing the *shofar* [ram's horn] on the High Holidays were reinstated.

Immediately before World War II, the congregation was primarily German Jewish, with many members related to the founders. But this was to change radically as those of Eastern European descent began to move from the North End to West Hartford. Rabbi Harold S. Silver, who succeeded Rabbi Feldman, describes the transition period after the war.

Rabbi Harold S. Silver.

# The Pioneer Synagogues

*The congregation had significantly started to dwindle, as had most of the old-line German classical Reform temples* [in the United States]. *In 1945, the congregation was no more than two hundred and fifty or three hundred families. After World War II, those who came into the Reform movement and into the Beth Israels of America were Jews who came from Eastern Europe, who had come at the turn of the century, who didn't want Orthodoxy. In the late forties and early fifties, and even into the sixties, these Eastern European Jews began to flood the old line German Reform congregations, and that resulted in the enormous growth of the new Reform movement, so by the sixties, a congregation like Beth Israel all of a sudden became fifteen hundred families—with over a thousand children in the religious school—overwhelming the small original Germanic group and moving the congregation into what we would call the more mainstream, liberal America.*

*When I came in 1968, the German Jewish leadership, which had predominated, began to disappear. They were passing away and being replaced by the Eastern European Jews who began to take the leadership roles and attempted to adjust to new Jewish forms of life and activity and involvement. They responded to it enormously in all kinds of ways.*

*My primary task in the early years was to institute all kinds of changes that would bring the congregation into the new mainstream Reform. For example, when I came, social action committees had never been formally a part of the institution. One of the first projects we helped to institute—my wife was enormously active in getting this project started—was an inner-city tutorial program at the Barnard-Brown Elementary School in Hartford. We were able to gather enormous numbers of volunteers to participate, not just within the congregation, but to reach out into the community and to try to be helpful there. That was something brand new.*

*One of my first acts was to change Confirmation from ninth grade to tenth grade in an attempt to keep the young people involved at least for another year, and then to develop what had never really been developed in the Reform movement, high school education for Jewish youth. So that was a big change locally. Teenagers were not represented in any of the committees of the congregation or on the Board of Trustees, and I wanted to get the young people involved in all facets of Jewish life. Confirmation was the be all and end all, and you really had to push to have a Bar Mitzvah. Shortly after I came, we instituted the first Bat Mitzvah where young women turning thirteen had the same privileges of going through the ceremony.*

The next shift in demographics at Beth Israel began in the late 1970s with the arrival of several hundred Jews from the Soviet Union. Separated from their religion by decades of Soviet policy, they knew little of Judaism and nothing of the American Reform movement that had "modernized" the ancient traditions. By the mid-1990s, nearly two thousand Soviet Jews had settled in central Connecticut. Said Rabbi Silver:

> *When the Russian Jews started to flock here to the United States and here to Greater Hartford, most of them originally settled in and around the Temple on Farmington Avenue, and we made a tremendous outreach to bring them in to the Temple, and it was a very exciting welcome for them. We organized classes and began to teach them English. We wanted to get them in, and primarily also we wanted them to enroll their children in the religious school because they had no opportunities in Russia for this. We realized that they couldn't afford the normal membership dues, which we waived. We just wanted them in and active and involved. The welcome was just open and warm. One of the things that saddened me somewhat is that not too many of the Russians who joined the congregation and were thrilled to be here and take advantage of this socially and culturally, not as many as we hoped enrolled their children in the religious school. But at least we knocked ourselves out to welcome them and make them feel like they were first-class members. I would say that not only in New England but probably nationwide, proportionally Beth Israel to this day has the largest component of Russian Jewish families who are full members. Today in 2006 we have about 1,250 total membership, and of those, 200 are Russian Jewish families.*

When Rabbi Silver retired in 1993, his assistant, Rabbi Simeon Glaser, took over the pulpit. In 1997, he was succeeded by Rabbi Stephen Fuchs who has become a spokesman for the Jewish community as a whole, teaching courses at St. Joseph College and the Hartford Seminary, writing for a variety of publications, and speaking out against anti-Semitism.

## Beth David Synagogue
### 20 Dover Road

In 1943, when the West Hartford Hebrew Committee met to discuss the possibility of founding an Orthodox synagogue and Hebrew school in West Hartford, Congregation Beth Israel was already established in the neighborhood. It did not, however, meet the needs of Orthodox Jews who adhered to the traditional ways. The following year the group purchased the

# The Pioneer Synagogues

Bishop mansion a few blocks west of Beth Israel, and in 1945 changed its name to the West Hartford Jewish Center. Calvin Mass said:

> *I belong to Beth David. My two brothers belonged to Beth David. I think I am the oldest continuous member of Beth David today. I've been paying dues continuously since 1946. I got through three building drives. The building started as a white house on the corner of Farmington Avenue and Dover Road. The property was bought by a few people, mainly by Gabriel Levine and the Rosensteins, the silk people. They had a silk mill in Vernon. At first it was a synagogue and social center for Jews. Rabbi Cohen was the rabbi for many years. There were two before him. When I joined, Rabbi Gordon had just left in 1946, and Rabbi Cohen had just been chosen. Back in the fifties, I was the president of the Brotherhood. I went through all the offices, and I eventually became the president of Beth David for three years in the 1970s.*

Rabbi William Cohen, who had graduated from Yeshiva University and then was ordained at the Rabbi Isaac Elchanan Theological Seminary, was part of the new generation of rabbis who were educated in America and preached in English. One of his first tasks was to expand and enhance the Hebrew School program.

> *When I came to Beth David in 1946, people were moving to the suburbs, and the Jewish community was spreading out. Those were hard times*

*for the Orthodox movement, which thrives on a compact community, but we held the line…We were a very young congregation when I arrived. It seemed by the early eighties that we were growing old together. Then we started to attract young families—strong, active leaders who were helping Orthodoxy make a comeback.*[14]

By 1954, Beth David had constructed a new building on Farmington Avenue, retaining the original house for classrooms. Eleven years later, on the twenty-fifth anniversary of the founding of the synagogue, the congregation replaced the house with a new sanctuary.[15] Calvin Mass believes that over the years Beth David has drawn three separate types of new members to the neighborhood.

*There were a lot of the young Jewish tshuvas* [newly Orthodox families] *that returned* [to traditional practice]. *Many of them came from families that were more or less secular or from families that came to this country and were more in the Conservative manner. It's a Modern Orthodox shul, which is different than the European Orthodox with American Orthodox rabbis educated in the United States. At Beth David there are a lot of young people in their forties, fifties who are very knowledgeable, can read from the Torah, and are practicing. Some of them are professors at the University of Connecticut, at Trinity. The Attorney General and the young people and the old people all belong to Beth David.*

*When the Russians came to Beth David, they were accepted with open arms. We got Russian sidurs* [prayer books] *for them. There is one fellow in our shul. He's in his nineties and had lived through the Stalin era. He went to a chedar* [European Orthodox school for boys]. *He was one of the few Russians that was able to read Hebrew well. He goes on the bima and does the Shachris. He studied for seventy-five years. He would study at night where nobody could hear him or see him to remain Jewish, to keep his Hebrew up. Most of the Russians that come don't know Hebrew. Some of them know Yiddish.*

*Beth David is doing very well. There are a lot of Jews on Robin Road and in that section of town, off of Farmington Avenue and Asylum that come here. Beth David also fused with a shul in Bloomfield, Teferes Israel.*[16] *It succeeded because of the brilliant efforts of a woman attorney. Sharon Freilich was the lawyer who navigated the collaboration. Their rabbi, Rabbi Lindenthal, is actually now the Rabbi Emeritus of Beth David like Rabbi Cohen of Beth David so we now have two emeritus rabbis.*

# The Pioneer Synagogues

When Rabbi Cohen retired after fifty years of service, Beth David was the largest Orthodox synagogue in Greater Hartford. Rabbi Yitzchok Adler who became the new rabbi told the *Jewish Ledger*:

> *The key word is tradition. Ours is a heritage based on legitimate origins that help link one generation to the next. My intent is to work within the Jewish community, bringing reverence and continued viability and vitality to the traditions of Israel that have facilitated Jewish continuity... The synagogue can impact people in a favorable way. It is more relevant to their lives when they understand what is experienced. It is not enough to be just an institution. It must be relevant.*[17]

Rabbi Adler also administers the Kashrut Commission of Greater Hartford, serves as a *mohel* for ritual circumcisions, was a founder of the Hebrew High School of New England, and teaches in *Yachad*, the supplementary Jewish high school in West Harford.

## THE CONSERVATIVE SYNAGOGUES

Although the Emanuel Synagogue and Beth El Temple have been separate entities since the early 1950s when Beth El broke away to form a new synagogue in West Hartford, they share more than thirty years of history in Hartford. Established in 1919 as B'nai Israel, the first Conservative synagogue in Greater Hartford, the name was changed to the Emanuel Synagogue soon after. While Rabbi Leon Spitz and Rabbi Abraham Nowak officiated in the earliest years, by 1923 Rabbi Morris Silverman had become the synagogue's spiritual leader, a position he held until his retirement in 1960. In 1927 Rabbi Silverman presided over the move from what had originally been the North Methodist Episcopal Church on Windsor Avenue to the new synagogue on Woodland Street, both in Hartford; the inauguration of the Bat Mitzvah for girls in 1928; and the development of programs for children and young people, including the Junior Congregation and the Young People's League. Additionally Rabbi Silverman's *Sabbath and Festival Prayer Book*, published by his Prayer Book Press, was widely adopted within the Conservative movement.

His wife, Althea Silverman, brought an additional dimension to the Emanuel. An author of stories, plays, pageants, children's books, and co-author of the *Jewish Home Beautiful*, she also taught classes on Jewish topics, organized concert series for children in Hartford, did interfaith work, and served on the Hartford Board of Education where she successfully fought a proposal to move music classes to Saturday mornings.

The Emanuel Synagogue on Woodland Street in Hartford.

By the early 1950s, the Emanuel faced two interlocking problems that would eventually divide the membership. With more than a thousand families and eight hundred Hebrew school-aged children, lack of space was becoming a serious issue. Additionally, more than half the congregation lived in West Hartford.[18] As members deliberated the merits of expanding the Woodland Street building or constructing a new religious school in West Hartford, a group led by Arthur and Pearl Weinstein and Isidore and Mickey Savin became convinced that the move to the suburbs was inevitable. Others, however, were determined to remain in Hartford. Louise Kemler Kaufman remembers the debate.

> *There had been a discussion with a fraction group that was going to splinter off. I know that there was a sense of a big backstabbing going on. Originally they said they weren't going to break off, and then they did* [in 1952]. *It was a very big disappointment that they broke the synagogue in two, but I think in the end, they saw that there were Jews who were Conservative who wanted, maybe, a more modern place to worship. I*

*think they were just following the migration of Jews to West Hartford. When they built Beth El, that part of Albany Avenue was really on the fringe. I think Beth El had more of an assimilated sense about itself, maybe second generation Americans, maybe third generation Americans where the Emanuel somehow was just little more old school Conservative. Rabbi Kessler* [the new young rabbi at Beth El] *was like a movie star. I can remember him when I was a little girl. He was going skiing. He wasn't what you thought of. He didn't have the looks of Rabbi Silverman or Rabbi Nowak. He was modern, and people were drawn to that.*

## BETH EL TEMPLE
## 2626 ALBANY AVENUE

In 1953, even though Rabbi Silverman had encouraged the group from the synagogue that was seriously considering establishing a new Conservative synagogue in West Hartford to become a branch of the Emanuel, they purchased ten acres on Albany Avenue for the new building and at a meeting for prospective members at Tumble Brook Country Club in Bloomfield recruited 156 new members, most from the Emanuel.[19]

The Friends Meeting House in West Hartford hosted the first service for the new group in April 1954. When Beth El asked Rabbi Stanley Kessler to lead the congregation, he conferred with Rabbi Silverman of Emanuel before accepting the position. Although both synagogues originally agreed to a joint religious school, this faltered after two years. Several years later, however, they collaborated on a highly successful high school program.

The Beth El building, dedicated in 1955, housed classrooms, offices and the vestry, which was used as the sanctuary. As the congregation grew, the need for more space became acute. In 1963, the new sanctuary opened. Its architectural plan incorporated a twelve-sided building with twelve windows, representing the twelve tribes of Israel, and a round roof symbolizing a circle without end. Twenty-six years later, as part of its thirty-fifth-anniversary program, Beth El dedicated a small chapel and on its fiftieth anniversary renovated the synagogue and enlarged the sanctuary.

As one of his earliest innovations at Beth El, Rabbi Kessler included women in the *minyan*, counting them among the group of ten necessary for many services and encouraging them to participate in the Torah service. Although this departure from tradition was not accepted by the Conservative

Arthur Weinstein, Rabbi Stanley Kessler, Joseph Kane, Leon Sondik and Simon Cohen participate in the groundbreaking ceremony for the new Beth El Temple in 1954.

Dedication of Education Building 1955 (left to right): Rabbi and Mrs. Kessler, Mrs. Silverman, Rabbi Silverman and speaker Harry Kleinman.

movement until 1973 when Beth El formally adopted it, at that point it had been part of the congregation's custom for nearly twenty years.[20] Rabbi Kessler was also concerned with discrimination and injustice in the wider world. He said:

> *During the Civil Rights era, there was a significant number of people who were opposed to what I was doing at the time. I was a Freedom Rider in Birmingham, Alabama during the riots there and in Selma. At a later time, I was on so many freedom marches in Washington so that some people, especially people who had property in the Northwest End, were very uncomfortable with what I was doing and for other reasons. Not everybody is as liberal in their feelings. So a lot of people were less than comfortable about where I was with Civil Rights, and I spoke publicly about it. But there was also a core group of people who were proud of what I was doing. I was given life tenure when I was here after ten years, and they could have made life very uncomfortable for me if they really felt there was too much of a gap between where their rabbinic leadership was and they were.*

After his retirement in 1992, as rabbi emeritus, Rabbi Kessler continued to pursue his interest in promoting peace and human rights. Following Rabbi Kessler was Rabbi James Rosen. Ordained at the Jewish Theological Seminary, he had served as the rabbi of Chizuk Amuno Congregation in Baltimore, Maryland before coming to West Hartford. A member of the Committee on Jewish Law and Standards of the Rabbinical Assembly, Rabbi Rosen is currently the President of the Connecticut Valley Rabbinical Assembly.[21]

From his position as the rabbi emeritus who is no longer involved in day-to-day work of the synagogue, Rabbi Kessler predicts further demographic changes as the population ages and younger families do not settle in West Hartford.

> *A lot of the old people are giving up their homes and going to condominiums* [and moving away]. *We have a very powerful group* [of senior members] *here at Beth El, the Chai Society. It represents a very, very significant part of the congregation at this point.* [And younger families] *are moving to the other side of the mountain. Twenty, twenty-five years ago, I urged our Board of Trustees to establish a* [presence] *on the other side of the mountain, but it never came about until after I left, and now there is a Simsbury group, the Valley Connection. I really felt that this was where the future is.*
> 
> *I think it would take another twenty-five or thirty years before* [this population shift] *touches* [our building] *in terms of that group*

*wanting to have their own school out there or having their own services out there. I'm not a prophet or a son of a prophet, but as I see what's happening, we are moving westward. I think that campus [which houses all of the Jewish community services in West Hartford] will be there for a hundred years, given the fact that mobility is so easy. It's only twelve minutes or so from Avon or Simsbury over to here by car. The big issues have to do with what happens in terms of the synagogue itself. I think that's a more difficult issue than the JCC or the home for the aged or the hospital that's developing with the Hebrew Home or other such matters. There are going to be some radical changes in how people will want to be rooting themselves.*

## The Emanuel Synagogue
### 160 Mohegan Drive

Third generation member of the Emanuel, Louise Kaufman recalls her father's stories about the early days of the synagogue and her own lifelong involvement with the Emanuel. Her children are fourth generation members. She said:

*I grew up with my father—R. Leonard Kemler—going to minyan [services] often. He grew up with the Emanuel literally. He was born the year the Emanuel was founded which was 1919. His father was one of the founders. It was the new Conservative movement that took hold in the United States, so we always had a real deep connection to that. My father was about thirteen when Louis Kemler died, so the Emanuel itself really became a family for my father. His mother died when he was four so the Emanuel was really like his home. Back then the synagogue was more social. Everything kind of went on there. It was right across the street [from Weaver High School] by Keney Park. It was really their world.*

 *It got to the point [in 1958] where [many members] felt that as suburbia was growing, and they were going to open a school [in West Hartford]. It wasn't the synagogue really. It was the educational aspect that moved, the Hebrew School and Sunday School. I guess the young families moving to West Hartford [were saying], "I can't bring my kid down to Hartford for Hebrew School twice a week." I went to Sunday School. When we got older, we had Hebrew School, which back then was two times a week so I would be there three times a week at a minimum. I would go from King Philip School right over there. Mrs. Missan was the*

# The Pioneer Synagogues

The new Emanuel Synagogue in West Hartford. "The Emanuel used to have this huge wall of blue and white glass. It was in the shape of menorah, and the sun would shine through that big stained glass wall. It wasn't great work of art, but I remember feeling really badly that they bashed that down." —Louise Kaufman

*head secretary, and she was very strict, and we all obeyed her. Mr. Weisel, he kept a firm hand on everyone. Mrs. Rubenfeld was my teacher. I thought she was so glamorous. Hebrew School was from four to six, Tuesday and Thursday or Monday and Wednesday and then on Sundays.*

*When I was a real little girl, what is now called Silverman Hall was our sanctuary. We sat on temporary seats that were set up. This was in the West Hartford building. Services had already ended in the Hartford building. The big thing was to build a new sanctuary [in 1970]. That was a huge undertaking for them, financial, construction. Back then there were men, families who were the real go-to guys. If the synagogue needed a roof, there were certain key families that they could go to, who offered tremendous support, financial support, like Butch Savin. If he wasn't going to raise it all himself, he knew who to go to. Back then you had the guy who owned the steel company, the guy who owned the lighting company, the roofing company, the heating. They all gave of themselves to the new building.*

*They enlarged the school wing. It was a long project, and it cost a lot of money. They used the brown brick, not really because it looked so great, but that's what they could buy. Everything about it was economical. The auditorium is the same building it was, and they opened up the sanctuary in front of it. But the real crowning glory of the new building was the chapel. They took the beautiful old stained glass windows from Woodland Street and brought them to the chapel. A few of them still remain in the sanctuary. When they had the fire, they were all ruined. They were all broken and ruined.*

In 1983, an arsonist set four fires in West Hartford. The first destroyed a Torah at the Young Israel on Albany Avenue and damaged the newly constructed synagogue building. The second fire, at the Emanuel in which seven Torahs and the chapel were destroyed, caused more than a million dollars' worth of damage. Two more fires damaged homes: that of Young Israel's Rabbi Solomon Krupka and that of Louise's parents, Leonard and Joan Kemler, who was the local state representative. Although the community feared an outbreak of anti-Semitism, the culprit was a troubled Jewish teenager, who was sentenced to probation and psychiatric therapy.

Since the 1960s, following Rabbi Silverman's retirement, Rabbi Simon Noveck, Rabbi Howard Singer, Rabbi Gerald Zelermyer and Rabbi David Small have led the Emanuel. Although the congregation is large, currently numbering about seven hundred families, its goal is:

*to be a synagogue that feels like a small shul. We approach our Congregation as an extended family. While many of our households are married couples with school-age children, the Emanuel is an inclusive and respectful, non-judgmental synagogue community where everyone is welcome. Seniors, singles, empty nesters, intermarried families, single parents, gays and lesbians and people with disabilities find a spiritual home at the Emanuel. Prayer, Torah study, helping others and performing acts of tikun olam (social justice) help us to grow closer.*"[22]

Chapter Three

# "It got so we all moved out— all of us."

—Rabbi Abraham M. AvRutick, Agudas Achim

## The Orthodox Synagogues

Between 1967 and 1976, five Orthodox synagogues—all but one with roots in Hartford—opened in West Hartford. In previous years, the majority of the Jews had been pulled out of Hartford by the promise of better housing in new suburban neighborhoods, but by the late 1960s, the anger of African Americans in the cities nationwide had begun to play out in Hartford and provided significant motivation for the remainder to leave. Among those were the Rothenbergs who had settled in the North End in 1952. Arriving as refugees after the Holocaust, Lottie and her husband had found work in the city, and their son flourished at Weaver High. Later they became part of the national trend toward "white flight." She said:

> [Our] *uncle sent papers. We had friends from the DP* [displaced persons] *camp that came to Hartford, and we were in touch with them. It was a good choice. We liked Hartford very much. Then the sixties came, and the schwartzes* [literally, blacks] *came. The whole neighborhood changed. When the troubles started* [in the late 1960's], *we moved* [to West Hartford]. *The synagogues moved too. Agudas Achim moved and Young Israel.*

## United Synagogues
## 205 Mohawk Drive

Like many of the early synagogues in Hartford, those that would eventually form the United Synagogues were small Orthodox congregations predicated on the traditions of the particular towns in Europe where their founders had originated. Over time, as the immigrants adjusted to life in America, European differences became less divisive, the membership changed, and the cost of maintaining a synagogue increased, leaving small congregations either to close or merge. The first of the three mergers that would ultimately become the United Synagogues took place in 1921 when Shaarey Torah (founded in 1887) and Ohave Zedek (1906) joined Beth Hamedrash Hagadol (1908). Although the latter retained its name, when the merged congregation moved to 370 Garden Street where it remained for forty-four years, the new entity was affectionately called the Garden Street *shul*.

In 1955, Congregation Ateras Israel (1895) absorbed Congregation Israel of Koretz, also called Anshe Koretz (1898). Under the name Ateras-Knesseth Israel, the new synagogue in 1954 hired Rabbi Isaac C. Avidgor, a young Holocaust survivor. He said:

> *The two congregations were merged, and upon merger decided to hire a rabbi. I was their first rabbi. It was a very difficult period because it was my first American position, and then it was a position in a merged congregation because the confrontation of the two different synagogues, the different personalities, the clash of cliques, which is usually true even in an original organization, was especially true when it was merged.*
>
> *After a few years, our area deteriorated, and we saw the handwriting on the wall that we must leave. We had a hundred and fifty children in the Enfield Street synagogue when my wife and I came down there, and within a period of three or four years, we were down to twenty-five, twenty-seven children. That was when we decided to purchase our new location on Mohawk Drive and North Main Street. But we didn't have the strength, the financial backing to start construction.*
>
> *At that moment, the Garden Street synagogue became vacant. Rabbi Singer had left it. We initiated a merger of these two synagogues. It was like marrying off two hundred couples. And here was yet a more difficult task because we had* [two different traditions, Sephardic and Ashkenazi]. *There was a newer synagogue on Enfield Street.* [Garden Street] *was an old building without classes, without structure, without a nice lawn. And what was most difficult for me to live with was the fact that the merged congregations decided not to proceed with construction in West Hartford. Instead of joining forces and go out right away and relocate as quickly as possible, the tendency was in the other direction.* [Eventually, construction began, and the United Synagogues moved into its new building in West Hartford in 1967.] *This is a conglomerate of five different synagogues, and this was symbolically emphasized by the architect by superimposing five stars, one on top of the other, to underline,*

## "It got so we all moved out—all of us."

The new United Synagogues building north of Bishops Corner.

*to underscore the five different synagogues under one roof. This was the merger.*[23]

By the time of Rabbi Avigdor's retirement in 1993, the aging membership had declined, and by 1996, the remaining families could not afford to maintain the building. After its sale to the Intensive Education Academy, United purchased and renovated a house around the corner on Mohawk Drive. Here the synagogue, under the direction of Rabbi Edward Cohen, has reconstituted itself as "a small intimate congregation with a very special Hebrew school…traditional, European style but energetic and warm and feely, a combination of what your grandparents observed and what a boutique synagogue ought to be."[24]

# Congregation Agudas Achim
# 1244 North Main Street

Agudas Achim, also called the Rumanisha Shul, or the Romanian Hebrew Congregation, was founded in Hartford in 1887 by immigrants from Rumania who were not comfortable with the Ashkenazi *nusach* [the pattern of the service] at Adas Israel, the only other Eastern European Orthodox congregation in Hartford. Accustomed to the *nusach sephard* as used by the Chassidim of Rumania, they preferred to worship in that pattern. Although its first rabbi, Isaac S. Hurewitz, was educated in the Lithuanian style, as were the founders of Adas Israel where he had served for several years before moving to Agudas Achim, he adapted to the *nusach sephard.*

In the early years, members of Agudas Achim met in homes and in one of its first acts established a cemetery where members could be buried at no cost. The congregation moved to Market Street between 1902 and 1903, remaining there until 1928, when it followed the Jewish exodus to the northwest section of the city. Rabbi Hurewitz was one of the founders of the Hartford Hebrew Institute, also known as the Pleasant Street Talmud Torah; of the United Jewish Charities and of the Union of Orthodox Rabbis of the United States and Canada. Beginning in 1909, he published a Yiddish newspaper, *Die Yuddishe Shtimme*, "the Jewish Voice." During Rabbi Hurewitz's tenure in Hartford, both the city and the Jewish community were changing with the native language of the new generation now English. Having an English-speaking rabbi had become a serious issue for some members who resigned and joined the Emanuel when Rabbi Hurewitz continued to preach in Yiddish.

Rabbi Hurewitz was followed by Rabbi Irving Weinberg (1935–1939), Rabbi Philip Greenstein (1939–1946), and in 1946 Rabbi Abraham N. AvRutick who served the Congregation for the next thirty-six years. Although Rabbi AvRutick was born into a Yiddish-speaking household in Russia, his family had immigrated to Montreal where he was educated in French and English. After graduating from Yeshiva College in New York, he studied at the Rabbi Isaac Elchanan Theological Seminary of Yeshiva University, which ordained him as a Rabbi in 1936. Said Leon Chameides, past present of Agudas Achim:

> *Under Rabbi AvRutick's leadership the congregation saw its greatest growth and became one of the largest and leading congregations in Connecticut. The Congregation recognized Rabbi AvRutick's leadership on his tenth anniversary (1956) when it gave him life tenure. Rabbi AvRutick's knowledge and leadership were recognized nationally when he received an honorary doctorate from his alma mater, Yeshiva University (1966) and when he was elected President of the Rabbinical Council of America, the umbrella organization of Orthodox Rabbis in the United States and Canada, in 1962.*[25]

Congregation Agudas Achim moved to North Main Street in West Hartford in 1969, and in the mid-1970s, Rabbi AvRutick said:

"It got so we all moved out—all of us."

Agudas Achim in Hartford.

"I always cry inside of me when I pass by my former synagogue. I loved that synagogue on Greenfield Street. I loved it. Number one, the structure: when you walked through that synagogue, you really felt you were walking on *makom kodesh*, into a holy place. This modern synagogue doesn't give you that warmth that you feel when you are walking into a really holy place." —Rabbi Abraham N. AvRutick

Agudas Achim in West Hartford.

> *I find my members no longer live in the environs of the synagogue. They're spread all over: West Hartford, Bloomfield, Windsor, Newington. It's a different kind of relationship. In former years, most of the people lived right around the synagogue. Now it's unfortunately not so.*[26] *The disintegration of a neighborhood plays havoc with the Orthodox synagogue, more than with the Conservative or Reform. When the neighborhood changes, it hits the whole gamut of the organized synagogues; the mobility of the population and the distance of living, worshipping, keeping Shabbos, a minyan, all of these things become of great importance to an Orthodox synagogue. And hence, these are very serious problems.*[27]

Dr. Chameides reflected on Agudas Achim at the end of the twentieth century.

> *The move to West Hartford was not kind to the congregation. Its members became older, and its location, some distance from the center of Orthodox settlement, saw a decline in its membership. On Rabbi AvRutick's death in 1982, he was succeeded by Rabbi Joshua Berkowitz who had been recruited as his Associate Rabbi in 1980. When Rabbi Berkowitz moved to California in 1988, he was succeeded by Rabbi Eric Kaye from Capetown, South Africa. Rabbi Jonathan Rosenbaum, the Maurice Greenberg Chair of Judaic Studies at the University of Hartford, next served the Congregation (1992–1998) as a part-time Rabbi. Rabbi Shlomo Yaffe became the congregation's spiritual leader in 1998.*[28]

## Young Israel of Hartford in Hartford

According to Mark Trencher and Sherry Haller in their 2006 history of Young Israel of West Hartford, the two Young Israel synagogues shared a common history in Hartford until they moved to West Hartford where they opened synagogues in different neighborhoods.

> *In 1935, Herman Eisenberg formed a Hartford branch of the national Young Israel synagogue movement with a group of young adults from the area. Its initial meeting was held at the home of Mr. and Mrs. Samuel Goldman, and for the first few years the group conducted its services in various area homes. As the group grew, services were held in the vestry of Agudas Achim Synagogue every Shabbat and on holidays.*

# "It got so we all moved out—all of us."

Young Israel of Hartford on Blue Hills Avenue.

*In 1943, many of Young Israel's members entered the armed services and the initial group was disbanded. However, in October 1945, a new group, which had also been worshiping in the Agudas Achim's vestry, purchased a residence at 191 Westbourne Parkway and converted it into a house of worship. Mr. Charles M. Batt served as spiritual advisor and Mr. Samuel Hoffenberg served as Chairman of the Board. The Women's League of Young Israel was also formed in 1945. The shul was a vibrant part of Jewish community life, and over the years it grew. To accommodate this growth, construction of the new building on Blue Hills Avenue was begun in November, 1962.*

*By the late 1960s Hartford, like many cities throughout the United States, was undergoing a transition. Many Jewish families were moving to the suburbs of West Hartford and Bloomfield. In anticipation of the impact this was going to have on the Young Israel, several members of the congregation began looking for a site in West Hartford. A property on Albany Avenue, consisting of an old house and nursery, was purchased. The first services of this new synagogue, the Young Israel of West Hartford, were held on March 28, 1968.*

> *By 1973, the Hartford Jewish community's neighborhood had changed to the point where the Young Israel of Hartford had to sell its Blue Hills Avenue building. Nearly all of its members moved to West Hartford, but many were not within walking distance of the West Hartford shul. As a result, the Young Israel of Hartford relocated in 1974 to its current location on Trout Brook Drive...The proceeds of the sale of the Blue Hills Avenue property were divided between the two branches.*

## Young Israel of West Hartford
## 2240 Albany Avenue

Even though a portion of the congregation had remained in Hartford, by 1978 the forty-five families living in West Hartford had replaced the house with a new synagogue building. In 1982, when the membership reached sixty families, the congregation hired Rabbi Solomon Krupka, who also taught at the Hebrew Academy, as the part-time spiritual leader. Until then, a rotating group of rabbis, members of the congregation, had conducted services.

In the summer of 1983, the sanctuary of the new building was destroyed in the first in a series of fires in the West Hartford Jewish community. Devastating for the Young Israel community was the knowledge that the arsonist was the disturbed son of a member family. According to then synagogue president, Mark Trencher, "We didn't miss a beat. Our own members and many others in the community rallied to our support. In three days, the entire *shul* was moved downstairs to the social hall, and everyone pitched in to begin the process of rebuilding."

When Rabbi Krupka moved to Israel the following year, he was succeeded by Rabbi Martin Rosenfield, a Connecticut assistant attorney general, who was active in the larger Jewish community where he chaired the Greater Hartford Rabbinic Fellowship, established the Kashrut Commission of Greater Hartford, and helped develop the *eruv*. Ten years later Rabbi Rosenfield accepted a position in Chicago. At that point, the congregation hired its first full-time rabbi, Rabbi Daniel Cohen, who was instrumental in bringing new young families into the synagogue. In 2002, when Rabbi Cohen left to become the leader of a large congregation in Denver, he was followed by Rabbi Howard Wolk, who resigned in 2006.[29]

"It got so we all moved out—all of us."

Members of both Young Israels practice for a Purim comedy, *South of Shushan*, a takeoff on *South Pacific* for a joint Purim party. Front row, left to right: Blumi Gelb, Sally Gelb, Rose Karpman and Shoshana HaCohen. Back row: Sol Sandlow, Moshe Weinberg, Ernest Feder, Fred Lipkind and Sam Sobel. *Photograph courtesy of Sally Gelb.*

## Young Israel of Hartford
## 1137 Trout Brook Drive

Fifty years ago, newlyweds, Ernest (Blumi) and Sally Gelb joined the Young Israel of Hartford, a move that continues to frame their religious life. Blumi is the *gabbai*, ensuring that the services run properly, and Sally is one of five generations of her family who have been connected to the synagogue building on Trout Brook Drive since the 1930s when her uncle, I. Oscar Levine, built it for his family home. She recalls the move from Hartford and the development of the synagogue.

> *One Shabbat, from the bimah, Paul Sava, then president of the synagogue, asked us to consider being trailblazers for the Young Israel of Hartford to the Fern Street section of West Hartford. This area was chosen for its similarity to the Blue Hills area. Both had lovely single homes, spacious flats and welcoming apartments. This would make it possible for people, some of whom were founders and members of the original Young Israel, to relocate according to their needs.*

*The first services of the transplanted synagogue were held on Shavous, 1970 in the Gelb living room. Larry Friedman volunteered to custom build an Aron Kodesh [ark] which could easily be moved, and Peggy Gurock made a lovely blue velvet curtain. The portable synagogue rotated from house to house every three weeks. The moving was an exciting event for the youngsters, who eagerly helped. It also taught them that it is not the walls that make a place of worship but what is contained within them.*

*Mike Sokoloff, president of the Young Israel of Hartford, was involved in the sale of the Blue Hills Avenue synagogue and was one of the guarantors on the loan for the purchase of 1137 Trout Brook. Noah Gurock played a major role in obtaining zoning permission, and Ernest Gelb was the shul's first president. Rabbi Charles Batt, continued as rabbi of the synagogue. He served, as have most, in a voluntary capacity. The membership included the rabbeyim of the Hebrew Academy and other young men steeped in Jewish learning, and they took turns giving weekly sermons and classes. Rabbi Gershon Brounstein, a gifted Torah scholar, continued to give his erudite Sabbath morning Germorah class. The little shul with a big heart continued to attract a wonder mix of people. The shul was known (and still is) for its home hospitality.*[30]

Over time, however, the Young Israel's membership has dwindled. The neighborhood is no longer a magnet for young Jewish families; members have relocated to Monsey—a religious community near New York City—or to Israel; and some have died. Even so, a new group of Soviet Jews attend the minyans, Shabbat services, and early morning *Daf Yomi* Talmud class. From 1999 to 2001 Rabbi Shlomo Yaffe served as the shul's spiritual leader, a position currently held by Rabbi Howard Wolk.

## Chabad House of Greater Hartford
## 2352 Albany Avenue

The Chabad House of Greater Hartford is linked to the Chabad Lubavitch Chassidic movement and is one the approximately thirty-five thousand Chabad centers around the world. Based on the teachings of the Baal Shem Tov, (Rabbi Israel ben Eliezer (1698–1760), Chabad Lubavitch was founded by Rabbi Shneur Zalman in what was then the Russian Empire. Although Chabad in the Soviet Union had been virtually destroyed by both the Communists after the Revolution and the Nazis during World War II, in 1940, the Rebbe, Rabbi Joseph Isaac Schneersohn, escaped to the United States, where he created a new center in the Crown Heights section

"It got so we all moved out—all of us."

In 1988, when the Chabad House opened, Rabbi Gopin (sixth from the left), hosted a dedication and conference. Rabbi Gopin sits between David Chase (left) and Harold Moffie and Rabbi Isaac Avigdor (right), all of West Hartford.

of Brooklyn. In 1951, he was succeed by his son-in-law, Rabbi Menachem Mendel Schneerson, who further revitalized the movement and continued to develop the system of emissaries, young couples who staffed Chabad houses in communities around the globe.[31] In 1977, Rabbi Joseph Gopin, his wife Miriam, and their baby daughter, Mina, became the emissaries in West Hartford.

> *We rented an apartment on Maplewood Avenue. It was our house, our office, our center, our meeting place. My first concentration was in University of Hartford, working with Jewish students, organizing Jewish events, holiday events, Friday night services, classes. In 1979, we also started a small day camp in the Granby area. In January of 1980 we bought a building on Farmington Avenue, a one-family house, converted to a small Chabad house for services, for classes, for meetings. We expanded the work to the University of Connecticut in Storrs, and we hired a new rabbi whose activity was to work with the college kids at the University of Hartford and UConn.*
> 
> *Chabad House got more involved in the community itself from 1980, developing more community programs, holiday programs, Shabbat services and programs, Friday night and holiday dinners, and many outreach*

# Jewish West Hartford

Campers from the Gan Israel Day Camp gather on the front steps of the Chabad House. *Photograph courtesy of Chabad House.*

*programs and lectures. After a while, we realized that the building is too small, and the Town of West Hartford also did not like us to be in that small little building. They really pushed us for a while to move out of there. We were lucky enough that Mr. Gabriel Levine, of blessed memory, in 1985, donated the land at Albany Avenue to us. We moved in here on Passover of 1988, having the first big seder in this Chabad House, and since then Chabad has been growing, developing better and more programs because we have more space, better space and are more centrally located in the community. We got more recognition in the community.*

*Our focus is different* [from other synagogues]. *Most synagogues wait for them to come to you, but we are proactive in going out to college kids, young families, old families, all ages, children. We are not waiting for them to come to us. We are going out, giving them a chance to educate themselves, giving them a chance to know better who they are and what's their relationship with their heritage and their history. Most people are unaffiliated Jews. A very big number of our students and supporters are people who do not belong anywhere, and* [we are] *their only Jewish connection.*

## "It got so we all moved out—all of us."

*A lot of people belong to other synagogues, and when they look for some more learning, they look for more inspiration, they come here, but they're not encouraged, in no way, to abandon their synagogues. We want then to continue where they are but to be more involved, more committed, more enriched. My experience though is that when those people go back to their synagogues, they are implementing a lot of the ideas from the Chabad in their synagogues.* [Among these are Lunch and Learn programs, and] *a lot of synagogues have Friday night dinners as a result of Chabad doing it. When I moved to West Hartford, there was almost no adult Jewish education going on in the community. Today, almost every synagogue is doing adult education. Chabad were the front-runners.*

## Non-Traditional Groups

## Kehilat Chaverim

Kehilat Chaverim, a Jewish Community of Friends that began in the West End of Hartford in the late 1970s, now holds monthly Friday night Shabbat services at the Quaker Meeting House, Sunday School at the Watkinson School, High Holiday services at the Jewish Community Center, all in West Hartford, and other gatherings in members' homes in the area. Although Joan Walden was not at the initial meeting, she joined the group soon after.

*We started right after the group got together to try to save the Charter Oak Temple, which became the Charter Oak Cultural Center. Some of the people who were interested in saving the Temple* [were also] *interested in forming an alternative Jewish community. I believe Deanne Shapiro and Sue Ginsburg were early founders. One of the reasons it appealed to me was because I was a single mother. I couldn't find a synagogue that I felt welcome in. There* [were] *people who were married to non-Jews looking for a religious organization where they could be Jewish but their spouses or significant others would feel welcome. If you were a single person or a single parent, or if you were gay or lesbian, if you were brought up Jewish, if you were looking for a place to affiliate, but no place felt right—these are the people who came together.*

*I wanted to go some place where I could say kaddish, some place where I could memorialize my parents. That was my personal motivation, and my son was getting closer and closer to thirteen, and I wanted him to have a*

*Bar Mitzvah. These people showed up on my doorstep at just the right time for me, and I think a lot of people felt that way for different reasons.*

*We felt that we didn't want a rabbi. We didn't want a building. We didn't want a Torah. Frankly, I would have been happy with a Torah, but the problem that came up when you don't have a building is who schleps the Torah? It seemed wrong that you would keep a Torah in the trunk of a car. How do you deal with it in a way that's respectful? I felt it was a practical matter that having a Torah really meant having an ark and having a building. One of the reasons we didn't want a building was because we had observed from our childhoods that when you have a building, that becomes what you get together about. You've got to pay for the building. You've got to pay for the rabbi. You've got to pay for the repairs etc. etc. And we didn't want money to be our central reason for coming together or for preventing people from coming together.*

*Clearly there was a need and a desire to celebrate the major holidays in some fashion because most of us weren't. We wrote* [and led] *all our own services and borrowed from a lot of traditional prayer books, but for* [Yizkor, the memorial service on Yom Kippur], *we encouraged people to write a personal memory piece that they could then read at the service, and that became very healing for the person who was doing it and healing for the people listening.*

*Anyone who is interested is welcome, but we understand that we're just not for everyone. I think that at some stages in peoples' lives we might fulfill a need more than at other times. Membership is limited to one hundred families, the requirement being that one adult from each member family is required to do work on a committee. So that's how it functions. It's very self-selecting, and frankly it works a whole lot better than I would have ever imagined over time. It really has created exactly what it's name says, a community of friends.*

## P'nai Or of Central Connecticut

*P'nai Or*—Faces of Light—is part of the national Aleph, the Alliance for Jewish Renewal, movement, and its Rabbi, Andrea Cohen-Keiner, a founder of the West Hartford group, received her *smicha* (rabbinical ordination) from that organization in 1999. In addition to serving the forty to fifty households that meet at the Flagg Road United Church of Christ, she is the Director of the Interreligious Eco-Justice Network. She said,

> [Around 1990] *Yossi Grodsky became the Hillel director of University of Hartford. He ordained also in Jewish Renewal, and we decided to start*

## "It got so we all moved out—all of us."

Rabbi Andrea Cohen-Keiner (first row, second from the left) meets with P'nai Or's Rosh Chodesh women's group. *Photograph courtesy of Andrea Cohen-Keiner.*

*a Jewish Renewal minyan, a chavurah. It was co-led, flat management style. Everyone knew a song or dance or poem that they wanted to lead or bring. They were welcome to do so. That went on for quite a while, meeting in each other's homes. There are only a handful of P'nai Or groups that have buildings and full time rabbis. That's not the model.*

*When we first started, we were more a community of seekers. About half of our members right now, today, belong somewhere else, [but P'nai Or] meets a need for them that isn't met where they're currently going. At the beginning, that was even more pronounced. It was an affiliation of seekers that came together to support a spirited religious practice. We practice meditation. We use spiritual direction and a process which we call "spirit buddies." People check in with each other and practice praying for each other around certain issues. For about half of our membership, this is their shul. At this point, there are more households of every age. To me that feels really good. They see each other on the Shabboses that we don't have services. It's not an event situation where we see each other once a month. It really is a vibrant community for us.*

*Jewish Renewal, I call it "neo-Chassidism." We tap into the mystical theology and the depth of practice that Chassidim have. We sometimes call ourselves post-halachic or trans-halachic—I don't usually use that language because I don't think we really left halacha* [Jewish religious law] *because we are working with halacha in ways that are non-Orthodox. For example, I'm a rabbi in this movement—no beard, no peyus* [long sideburns worn by traditional Orthodox men]*—so obviously we ordain women. I think we have taken the best from each of the four movements. We've taken the social justice vision from the Reform. The deliberate dialogue, we've taken from the Conservative movement, where they deliberate over the ancient and modern criteria. We've taken the seriousness of practice from the Orthodox, and we've taken the depth of practice from the Chassidic.*

## The Minyan

In 1985, Phil Schlossberg, who was familiar with *chavurot* in the Boston area, approached Steven Chatinover, then rabbi of the Reform Beth Hillel in South Windsor, about putting together an informal group, which would meet once or twice a month to supplement the Shabbat experience. Convinced of the importance of belonging to a synagogue with a complete range of age groups and programs, Schlossberg saw the Minyan as an enrichment with in-home services run by the members, a potluck meal, and *zimrot* [Shabbat songs].

The Minyan started with a group of about a dozen families, most in their late twenties or early thirties, almost all of whom were well educated in Jewish topics, with Schlossberg himself a product of the Emanuel religious school, Camp Ramah and Brandeis University Hillel. In the early years, the Minyan met primarily on Saturday mornings for services, Torah readings and discussions, but over time, the Friday evening dinners have become more popular. Every year the Minyan hosts a lunch in the Schlossberg family Succah and occasional Shabbat singalongs. Although only a handful of the original families remain, membership is open with about twenty families on the mailing list.[32]

## FORMER GROUPS

## Sephardic Congregation of Connecticut

Even before its incorporation as the Oriental Brotherhood Hebrew Society in 1924, seven Turkish Jewish families in Hartford had been meeting in homes to pray according to the Sephardic liturgy. The original families—

those of Aaron Ben Maor, the first president; Victor Saul, who also served as president and cantor; Samuel Levy and David Sasportas, incorporators; and Abaye Cordova, Ambram Hatten, and Zakay Nathan—were descended from Jews who fled the Spanish Inquisition and settled in Turkey, where they spoke Ladino, a language derived from classical Spanish flavored by Hebrew and the languages of the countries around the Mediterranean where the Sephardim had settled.[33] According to Madalyn Levy, a descendant of a founding family and for many years the treasurer of the group and organizer of the High Holiday service:

> *The By-laws provided that members shall be admitted once they reach the age of 18 years. A married individual applying for membership must have celebrated marriage according to the Hebrew marriage law. A member later married would not be recognized as a member if his marriage was not according to Hebrew law. Applicants were charged an admission fee of two or three dollars, depending upon age. Weekly dues were ten cents per member, and five cents for the wife of a member. Benefits were available to members for physical disability or sickness. In case of death of a husband, wife, child or member, the Corporation paid the funeral expenses.*[34]

Over the years, the *Ermandad Sephardit*, as it was called in Ladino, held services in various synagogues in Hartford, moving to West Hartford in 1975 where members gathered for High Holiday services in the chapel of the Emanuel. During the remainder of the year, many belonged to larger Ashkenazi synagogues with religious schools for the children.

Although more than one hundred Sephardic families—from such diverse countries as Argentina, Cuba, Israel, Morocco, Lebanon, Iraq, Iran, Curacao, and Greece as well as Turkey—had relocated to Greater Hartford by the 1990s [35] and some attended the Sephardic High Holiday services, as a group they did not become members of what had become the Sephardic Congregation of Connecticut. In 2003, the services moved to Agudas Achim for two years, but as the Turkish congregation, which had traditionally organized the services, diminished, there were no longer enough members to form a *minyan*, and it disbanded.[36]

## Am Segulah

Am Segulah—the Chosen or Treasured People—was founded in 1984 by a small number of gay and lesbian Jews. The congregation met for Shabbat services and social events in Hartford and West Hartford homes. Recently, Am Segulah broke apart, with some members joining a synagogue in

Newington. While this segment of the group was interested in connecting with mainstream synagogue life, others were uncomfortable with this decision and continue to maintain their listing on the gay and lesbian websites in the hope that new people will contact them about reconstituting the group.[37]

## Ohavei Shalom

In 1989, a group from West Hartford and the surrounding communities formed Ohavei Shalom—Lovers of Peace—a *chavurah*-style synagogue, which emerged from the Minyan. While some of the members continued to attend their original synagogues and/or the Minyan, a number were otherwise unaffiliated. Many were parents of children who attended the Solomon Schechter Day School or in later years the Hebrew Academy. Led by volunteers, including Rabbi Steven Chatinover, the egalitarian group altered over time with many of the members joining Conservative and Orthodox synagogues with religious schools and youth groups. In 1992, Ohavei Shalom was invited to rent space in the Orthodox United Synagogues, an unusual marriage which lasted until United sold the building, and the group moved to Beth El as a recognized *chavurah*. Since then Ohavei members have either left Beth El for a variety of reasons or integrated into the mainstream of what is currently the largest Conservative synagogue in Connecticut.

## Chapter Four

# Community Service Agencies

With caring for the less fortunate and making the world a better place to live as cornerstones of the Jewish religion, it is not surprising that as the immigrants put down roots in Connecticut, they formed a variety of charitable organizations to assist the needy in Hartford and abroad. In addition, solicitors from what became known of as the "traditional institutions" in Europe and Palestine regularly knocked on doors asking for money. According to Betty N. Hoffman in her study of the Jewish Federation of Greater Hartford:

> *In 1912, three leading rabbis—Harry Ettelson, Chemach Hoffenberg, and Isaac S. Hurewitz—joined with influential lay leaders including Isidore Wise, as its first president, to unite thirty diverse groups into a single charitable association, the United Jewish Charities. During its first year, the new organization raised eight thousand dollars, which was spent on such varied activities as providing meals for transients, helping those with medical needs, making loans, and assisting the unemployed...Over time, the United Jewish Charities became more than just an umbrella organization formed to administer charitable funds more efficiently. It brought together disparate groups, providing through its activities a place where Jews from various backgrounds could meet on neutral ground.*[38]

As part of its effort to consolidate and streamline charitable giving and the provision of services during the late 1930s and early 1940s, the United Jewish Charities set up a series of new agencies for planning and fundraising. This process culminated in 1945 with the incorporation of the Hartford Jewish Federation under its first director, Bernard Gottlieb, a seasoned administrator experienced in Jewish community service. According to its Certificate of Organization, the goal of the new organization was:

> *To coordinate, promote, and advance the educational, cultural, social and philanthropic activities of the Jewish community; to raise and collect funds for distribution to and for the support of overseas, national and local Jewish nonprofit agencies; to undertake responsibility for central planning, coordination and administration of local Jewish Welfare services to help safeguard and defend the civic, political and religious rights of the Jewish people.*[39]

For more than half a century, a remarkable group of powerful and respected lay leaders, many of the them prominent businessman and professionals who lived in West Hartford, served as Federation Presidents and Campaign Chairmen. Founding president Edward A. Suisman (1944–1946) was well known for the large sums he raised for charity. According to his son Michael:

> *He became involved in Jewish philanthropy and ultimately the Federation because his mother and father were very active in Jewish life and in philanthropy. His mother Sarah P. Suisman was one of the founders of the Hebrew Home for the Aged and was involved in many activities. She herself went around in the early years with pushkes* [small containers for individual charities] *and raised nickels and dimes. My father learned from his mother and became active in the thirties and early forties in what would become the Federation. It federated all the fund raising in the Hartford area, and my father became the first president.*
>
> *There were a bunch of friends, the most important one I would say was his brother Samuel Suisman, and they were together for fifty years or more in business* [at Suisman & Blumenthal], *and Samuel Suisman was a great philanthropist himself. But my father took the front position, and he had a group of friends,* [among them] *Mel Title and Barney Rapaport, who was a major giver in those days, and this group of men were the ones that believed that the Federation had to be formed. It was a very unorganized kind of a situation in Hartford, and they saw that if they pooled all the fundraising under one umbrella that it would be much more efficient and ultimately raise far more money that way.*

Following Edward A. Susiman into the Federation presidency were his sons Michael who served as a two-term president (1970–1974) and Richard (1987–1989). Only two other families have had sons follow their fathers

## Community Service Agencies

Past presidents of the Federation (left to right) I. Oscar Levine (1950–1952), Abraham Bordon (1949–1950 and 1963–1964), Melvin Title (1948–1949), Edward Suisman (1947–1948), N. Aaron Naboicheck (1960–1962), Stanley Fisher (1958–1960), and Charles Rubenstein (1969–1970).

into the presidency of the Federation: N. Aaron (1960–1962) and Robert (2001–2003) Naboicheck and Charles (1969–1970) and Richard (2003-2005) Rubenstein.

Standing alone as the only woman to hold the positions of campaign chair, president, and chairman of the board of the Federation was Paula Steinberg, who moved from New Britain to West Hartford when she was a child in the 1940s. She said:

> *I became a volunteer very early, not necessarily in the Jewish community. Then in the eighties I started to work for the Federation, just doing small things. I was working on a dinner, working on a little bit of Super Sunday. I said I could never ask anyone for money. It wasn't until 1993 that I was asked to be a Major Gift Chair in the Women's Division. The next thing I knew Cindy* [Chazan, the Executive Director of the Federation] *and Rise Roth, who was then the Women's Chair, invited me to lunch—I knew I was in trouble—and they asked me to be the Women's Campaign*

Paula Steinberg is the only woman to have served as president of the Federation.

> Chair. It isn't just picking up the phone and asking someone for money. You have to be able to answer the questions. There are an awful lot of things you have to know.
>
> At the end of that period, the man who was the General Campaign Chair decided he wasn't going to do it for a second year, and I suddenly became the General Campaign Chair. No other woman had ever been General Campaign Chair. The campaigns had been slipping and slipping and slipping—this was right after the horrible eighties—but by the time I became the General Campaign Chair, it was 1996. Things were starting to get better. We went over $5 million for the first time in a very, very long time.[40]
>
> Being president was just an overwhelming thought because there had never been a woman. There were a lot of people who said to me, "You're never going to make it. It won't work. Nobody's going to give a big gift to a woman," things of that sort. In 2000—I was president during that year until November—my husband died. Some of the men assumed that I would not be able to function, so they were going to take over for me. I said, "I will mourn for my husband, and I will be appropriate. You don't have to take over for me. I am going to be all right." My husband was sick for a long time, and he wouldn't have wanted me to fall apart.

Over time, as the Federation has become the central and most influential organization in the Jewish community, it has brought the majority of Jewish

A YMHA and YWHA outing about 1923.

agencies and services into its fold. While a number of these had long histories in Hartford before moving to West Hartford, others developed in West Hartford after the bulk of the Jewish population had left the city.

## THE JEWISH COMMUNITY CENTER
### 335 BLOOMFIELD AVENUE

In 1962, the Jewish Community Center (JCC) was the first beneficiary agency of the Hartford Jewish Federation to move to West Hartford. Between 1878 and 1948, when the JCC was established under that name, seven organizations had provided recreational programs for immigrant youth in Hartford at different times with the Jewish Center Association, directed by George Gershel, opening in 1942.

Under the auspices of the United Jewish Social Service, the JCA had its headquarters in that agency's Vine Street building. As the JCA's programs grew in popularity, the small building was unable to accommodate them, forcing the JCA to rent space in schools and use public parks.

As the newly formed Hartford Jewish Federation began to plan for the future, it recognized the need to expand the Jewish Center Association. In 1948, the Federation's Three-Way Drive raised $1.5 million as part of its

## Jewish West Hartford

In 1961, (left to right) Saul Karovsky, Ezra Melrose, Anna Hoffenberg, Delott Garber, Aaron Naboicheck and Irving Stitch watched the groundbreaking ceremony for the new Jewish Community Center.

Walter Gropius and Norman Fletcher of the Architects Collaborative designed a $1.7 million building, which opened in the fall of 1962 and housed a state-of-the art theater; rooms for clubs, meetings and classes; a swimming pool and other recreation facilities and a nursery school. A renovated firehouse on the site became the home of the Federation.

## Community Service Agencies

After the move to West Hartford the walls of the Asylum Avenue Jewish Community Center in Hartford came tumbling down.

The JCC Purim Party in 1981 drew a large crowd.

# Community Service Agencies

larger capital campaign and purchased a building at 1015 Asylum Street for a new Jewish Community Center.[41] Four years later, the Jewish Children's Service Organization bought a camp in New Hartford, which it leased, to the JCC for a dollar a year.[42]

As JCC membership increased, proliferating programs for all ages were outgrowing the Asylum Avenue building. In 1959, the JCC bought land on Bloomfield Avenue in West Hartford from the Fire and Casualty Insurance Company of Connecticut. The following year, Archbishop Henry J. O'Brien and the archdiocese donated an adjacent parcel.

By 1970, 1,760 families—7,832 individuals—belonged to the JCC.[43] In 1977, the Federation and the Jewish Center Camping Committee purchased Camp Mar-Lin in Windsor and renamed it Camp Shalom. "The acquisition of our new camp facility," said JCC president, Jerry Wagner, "offers an unparalleled opportunity to serve the Jewish youth of the capitol region and to instill Jewish values in a beautiful and convenient setting."[44]

By the 1980s, the JCC's general programs included cultural programs, classes, sporting events and clubs for members of all ages. Additionally, by the end of the decade, the number of refugees from the Soviet Union began to increase, and the JCC became an important part of their resettlement process. In 1993, staff member Lucy Dravta started the Association of Invalids and Veterans of World War II of the Former Soviet Union in Greater Hartford. She also facilitates a cultural club and support group, Music by the Fireplace. Nina Aronov is one of the founders of the group.

> *The purpose of this club is for people* [to enjoy themselves], *to make their lives more interesting. We are including poetry, music, history, history of America, some stories, and people speak about their experience, about their lives, what they think, exchange opinions. We are communicating. It's very important. We give some advice to each other. We are dancing near the fireplace. It gives us warmth. We support each other.*

Mark Aronov, a retired physician, who found it difficult to adapt to life in West Hartford, reflected on the importance of the organization.

> *People who come from the former Soviet Union are isolated in this world because of their lack of English. When they come to this group and meet together, their lives become better because of this club.* [The members are] *intelligent educated people, physicians, scientists, artists, veterans, musicians, economists, who, when they came to the Untied States, could not*

# Community Service Agencies

Nina Aronov holds the microphone for Mayya Patent at a meeting of the Music by the Fireplace Club. Mayya said, "My aunt used to sing beautifully. It was before World War II, and I fell in love with her singing and beautiful music and how she performed. I try to copy this in my own performance when I sing the old-fashioned Russian songs." *Photograph courtesy of Lucy Dratva.*

*work any more, and they kind of lost themselves here. But when they came to this support club, they found themselves, and they enjoy it.*[45]

When the Federation's 1980s "Greater Hartford Jewish Population Study" indicated that the Jewish Community Center would need to expand yet again to meet future community needs, the JCC began a construction and renovation project that was completed in 1990. This added a new pool, improved the athletic center, and reconfigured the internal space to provide for a Holocaust room, an art gallery, archives for the Jewish Historical Society and offices for the Commission on Jewish Education, and an enlarged and improved space for the Beatrice Fox Auerbach Early Childhood Center.[46]

As the Jewish community slowly climbed out of the recession in the 1990s, the Federation inaugurated another long-range study that underlined the

Former Soviet army officer Lazar Grabarnik (left) is president of the JCC veterans organization. "We participate in all of the activities affiliated with the war veterans in West Hartford and Hartford, too. At the state of Connecticut capitol on Holocaust Day, May 6, we march together with American World War veterans, and in the Senate Chamber, we stay in front of the flag and salute the people who suffered from the Holocaust." Lucy Dratva is on the far right. *Photograph courtesy of Lucy Dratva.*

need for new or renovated buildings and enhanced endowments for thirteen of the Federation's beneficiary agencies. In 1999, the Jewish Community Center joined the Community Capital Campaign to raise funds for this massive project. The JCC's specific plan was to renovate its interior and to expand the facility. When the land adjacent to the Jewish Community Center became available, Henry Zachs, then Chairman of the Federation Board, and his family made its purchase possible. The Zachs Family also bought and renovated the Suburban Swim Club in Bloomfield for the JCC.

By the mid-2000s, construction was well under way for the newly renamed Joyce D. and Andrew J. Mandell Jewish Community Center and for the new Hoffman Field House. Saint Francis Hospital and Medical Center had signed on to operate an innovative health project and provide rehabilitation services in the new space. Among the new programs is the Family Room Parenting Center, a drop-in center with programming designed for families with young children.

## The Jewish Family Services of Greater Hartford
### 333 Bloomfield Avenue

As the Depression deepened and the refugee crisis in Europe increased in the late 1930s, new social security legislation out of Washington began to transfer part of the financial burden of supporting the poor from charities, such as the United Jewish Charities, to the federal government. This allowed the UJC to focus on family service, and in 1940, it changed its name to the United Jewish Social Service Agency (UJSS). Through its work with the local German Refugee Committee (formed in 1937) and its post-war connection with the United Service for New Americans, the Location and Migration Service of the UJSS resettled five hundred and sixteen Holocaust survivors in Connecticut by 1952.[47]

Although refugee service was the primary function of the UJSS immediately after the war, it began to combine a variety of programs previously run by other organizations into one centralized agency. By 1947, new methods of dealing with orphans and children unable to live with their parents made the residential facilities of the Hebrew Home for Children (founded in 1907) obsolete, and that agency merged with the UJSS. When adoption laws changed in the late 1950s, the agency took on the additional responsibility of placing Jewish children with adoptive families.[48] In 1950, the agency dropped the word "United" from its name and became the Jewish Social Service.

In addition to the full range of counseling services developed over time, the Jewish Family Service (JFS)—as it became in 1968—remained the agency responsible for resettling refugees: from Cuba during the 1950s and from the Soviet Union beginning in the mid 1970s. This focus on refugees would remain an important part of the agency's work throughout the remainder of the century.

In 1977, the Jewish Family Service moved to 740 North Main Street in West Hartford's Bishops Corner. Two years later, as the Soviet Union began to allow Jews to leave, the Federation, JFS, and local volunteer service organizations developed a strategy for resettling them in central Connecticut, primarily in West Hartford. At that time, Philip Weiner, Executive Director of the agency, noted that the JFS was "designed for small resettlement efforts. This will be a strain on the community and its agencies."[49]

Said Marvin Kay, the JFS social worker responsible for the resettlement program, "There was no [official] policy *per se* regarding these folks [other than that] I had to find housing for them. They were given allowances through Federation which also gave us a budget." Although the refugees

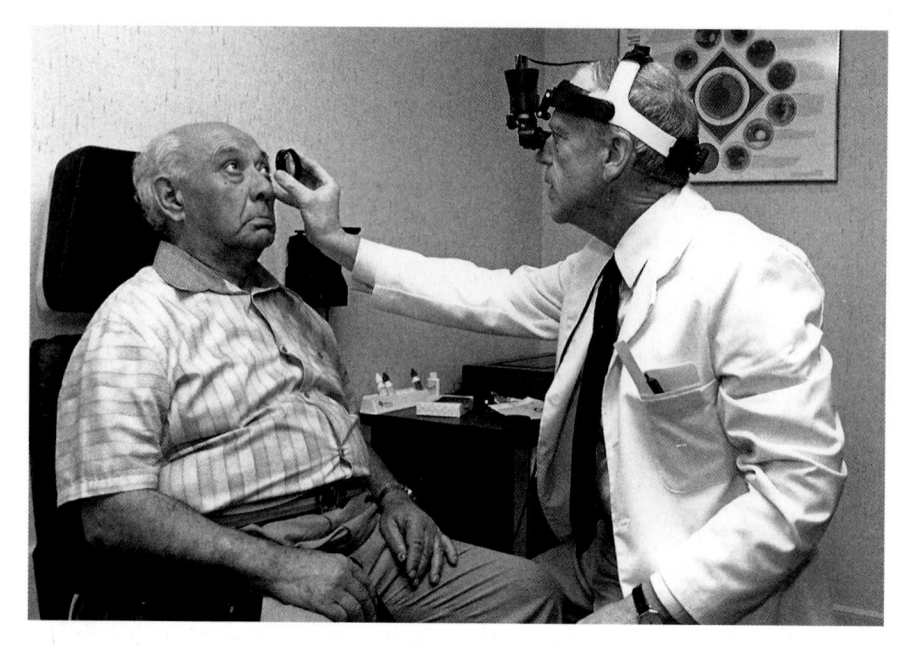

Dr. Felson examines the eyes of a refugee from the Soviet Union.

numbered fewer than two hundred and fifty in the first years, by the end of the 1980s, the numbers had increased substantially, until the mid 1990s when they dropped off again.

In the late 1980s and early 1990s, Vida Barron, the JFS Director of Resettlement, and her staff guided the second wave of New Americans through their early difficult days. As they had in the 1970s, local volunteers, many from the National Council for Jewish Women, ORT, and the synagogues joined with the Federation agencies to ease their transition to Jewish life in Connecticut. An estimated two thousand Soviet Jews have settled in the area with, at least initially, most in West Hartford.

By 2005, the Jewish Family Services had embarked on the development of new and expanded programs, on the implementation of its new strategic plan, and on meeting the Jewish Community Fund's challenge for the agency to raise endowment funds. JFS was also a partner in the Community Capital Campaign, which would provide modern office space in the new Community Services Building on the Zachs Family Campus.

The Jewish Family Services continues to offer counseling services to anyone who needs assistance in coping with every aspect and stage of life, provides a homemaker service for those who need help remaining in their homes, and distributes food from its kosher food pantry. According to its mission statement, the Jewish Family Services:

> *is dedicated to providing social services and mental health programming in a manner that fosters the core values of its primary client group, the Greater Hartford Jewish Community. All Jewish Family Services programs and services are available to the general community on a non-discriminatory basis. The agency is committed to the continuity of Jewish life and to its long tradition of servicing its clients in accordance with the highest professional standards.*[50]

## MIKVEH BESS ISRAEL OF WEST HARTFORD
### 61 NORTH MAIN STREET

In traditional Judaism, the *mikveh* or ritual bath plays a central role in Jewish life.

"According to Jewish law," said Rabbi Emeritus William Cohen of Beth David Synagogue in West Hartford, "the *mikveh* is considered of such prime importance that it takes precedence over the building of a synagogue or of the writing of a *Sefer Torah*."[51] Based on the ancient practice of ritual purification by complete immersion in water before entering the Temple in Jerusalem, the use of the *mikveh* today is a critical component of traditional family purity. It is also a core element in conversion. Every *mikveh* must adhere to specific Jewish laws including where it is constructed in the building, how much water it holds and how the water flows into the pool.

Although most Jews had left Hartford by the late 1970s, the *mikveh* of Hartford remained on Blue Hills Avenue, and its members continued to raise funds for its maintenance and hold meetings and social events. In 1976, however, an era came to the end with the death of the "*Mikveh* Lady," and President Jack Schuss told a large group at the *Mikveh's* twenty-fourth *Melava Malkah*—a festive meal at the end of the Sabbath—"There are day to day problems, but the ultimate answer is to move to West Hartford."[52]

Within eighteen months the group had established a building fund, purchased a house on North Main Street in West Hartford, and received permission from the Town to convert it into a ritual bath. In 1984, Congregation Bess Israel, which had closed in Hartford, retired the *Mikveh's* thirteen-thousand-dollar mortgage and opened a thousand-dollar endowment fund in exchange for the *Mikveh's* changing its name to *Mikveh Bess Israel* to memorialize the former synagogue. That same year the *Chesed Shel Emes* (Burial Society) funded replacing the windows, building a

# Jewish West Hartford

Bobby Shapiro; Marlene Scharr; Ellen Roisman, president of the JCL Auxiliary; Marsha Lotstein; and Patty Schuster stand in front of the new Arapahoe Road group home. Board member Bobby Shapiro was involved in setting up the home's kosher kitchen.

private entrance at the back of the building, and generally improving the property.[53] Governed by a volunteer board, *Mikveh Bess Israel* continues to offer its traditional services in West Hartford.

## Jewish Association for Community Living

In 1976, a Federation survey of the elderly in the community highlighted the need for supported housing, particularly for those with low incomes. As the Federation considered constructing senior citizen housing in Bishops Corner, Marlene Scharr and Sophie Mayron, West Hartford mothers of disabled young adults, lobbied for the inclusion of handicapped accessible apartments for those who needed assistance to live independently. Although named Federation Square, the complex—which opened in 1980 with nine of its eighty-eight apartments set aside for those with physical and/or mental handicaps—is not formally associated with the Federation.[54]

Additionally, a 1979 survey had found that at least seventy-five families in the region had members who were developmentally disabled. It was clear that more housing and support services were needed. Meanwhile, the Jewish Community Center and Camp Shalom were beginning to create social and recreational programs for those with disabilities.

In 1981, the Committee for the Developmentally Disabled changed its name to the Jewish Association for Community Living (JCL) and joined the Federation as a beneficiary agency. According to Chairwoman Marlene Scharr, the purpose was "to establish a variety of living opportunities for Jewish people who are disabled and to help integrate people with disabilities into Jewish community life."[55] Within months the JCL had raised enough money to buy a lot on Arapahoe Road in West Hartford Center and build a group home. The new building housed six disabled adults with a residential director and staff that provided twenty-four-hour supervision.[56]

Over the past quarter century, the JCL has continued to assist those with developmental disabilities by opening two more group homes, supervising those living in apartments, and providing counseling for families of clients. Although not all residents are Jewish, the JCL celebrates the Jewish holidays and supports Jewish traditions.

## Hebrew Health Care
## One Abrahms Boulevard
## Hoffman SummerWood Community
## 160 Simsbury Road

Hebrew Health Care is the oldest Jewish agency in Greater Hartford providing the same type of service to the community that it did more than one hundred years ago. What began with the Hebrew Ladies Sick Benefit Aid Association's purchase of a house at 33 Wooster Street in Hartford for five thousand dollars as a home for four elderly residents has become a multi-million dollar complex in West Hartford. It now encompasses the Gene and Anja Rosenberg Hebrew Home and Rehabilitation Center, the Hospital at Hebrew Health Care, Hebrew Community Services, the Hebrew Rehabilitation Group and the Hoffman SummerWood Community for assisted living.

Although the Hebrew Ladies renovated the Old People's Home in 1911, the needy elderly population continued to grow, and in 1919 the Ladies purchased a larger house at 276 Washington Street.[57] In 1945, the Hebrew Home for the Aged became one of the first agencies to join the new

Hartford Jewish Federation. Three years later, the home was one of the beneficiaries of the Federation's Three-Way Drive fundraising campaign for the construction of a larger facility. When the new $1.6 million home opened on Tower Avenue behind Mount Sinai Hospital in 1953, it had beds for two hundred residents, offices for auxiliary services, a library and a synagogue.[58] Its proximity to Mount Sinai Hospital played an important role in patient care.

Throughout the years, the Hebrew Home underwent renovations and expansions, and during the 1960s, it added a variety of clinics, occupational and physical therapy units, increased nursing care, and in 1969, the Sigel Wing, which provided rooms for forty-five more residents.[59] In addition to expanding its off-site clinics and Kosher Meals-on-Wheels, the Home opened an on-site adult day care. In the mid-1970s, the name changed to the Hebrew Home and Hospital to reflect the Home's new status as a chronic disease hospital and its affiliation with the University of Connecticut Medical School.

As the neighborhood changed, the Hebrew Home and Mount Sinai became isolated from their core Jewish population, which had moved to the suburbs. This fact, combined with the need to modernize and expand the Hebrew Home yet again, prompted plans for a new facility adjacent to the Jewish Community Center and the Federation in West Hartford. Said Irving Kronenberg, President of the Hebrew Home, in 1986:

**Under Construction**

"The Hebrew Home and Hospital will be a combination four-story and single-story brickface structure, totaling over 165,000 square feet. It will house 326 residents at three levels of care; and it will also provide adult day care services to approximately 60 clients per day…The location of our 25-acre site will enhance our abilities for shared, intergenerational programming with the Jewish Community Center next door."—Sandy Zieky and Judy Greenberg

*Meeting the needs of an increasingly frail population is a complex task. It is not enough to know what services are needed; we must also plan physical facilities which will support those programs and which will enhance both our services and the quality of life for our residents.*[60]

Construction began in 1986, and the first residents moved into the state-of-the-art building in December 1989.[61] Within ten years, however, the Hebrew Home had joined the Community Capital Campaign to update its facility and to build SummerWood at University Park, the first Jewish community sponsored kosher assisted-living facility in the region.[62]

Mount Sinai Hospital, the final Jewish agency to remain in Hartford, did not fare as well. Although Mount Sinai was providing critical medical services to the community, its financial position was precarious with increasing numbers of its patients dependent upon government insurance programs that did not pay the full costs of treatment. In 1989, the same year that the Hebrew Home left the city, Mount Sinai's president, Robert Bruner, negotiated a health care alliance with Saint Francis Hospital and Medical Center. With the merger complete in 1995, Mount Sinai closed its doors forever.

Chapter Five

# Social Structure

## JEWISH EDUCATION IN WEST HARTFORD

Although the Yeshiva of Hartford, an Orthodox day school, opened in 1940, it did not did not draw students from the majority of Jewish families who were committed to the public schools. While some families sent their young children to the supplementary classes at the individual synagogues, others paid little, if any, attention to religious education. By the early 1960s, the Emanuel and Beth El, the Conservative synagogues in West Hartford, had expanded their programs to provide advanced classes, and in 1963, joined with Beth Hillel in Bloomfield to open the Midrasha, a six-hour-a-week high school.

In the late 1960s, Alfred Weisel, a founder of the Midrasha, the educational director of the Emanuel Synagogue, and chairman of the Conservative Jewish Education Council, challenged the Federation's new Committee on Jewish Education to improve local Jewish education by instituting innovative programs and providing teacher training. When the Federation formed the Commission on Jewish Education, Weisel became a consultant and in 1985 it's full-time director.

At the end of 1972, the Federation's Self-Study Committee, chaired by Arnold C. Greenberg, began to examine the changing demographics and geography of the Jewish community. Its recommendations would create heated debate about the Federation's role in funding Jewish education. Greenberg said:

> One extremely important item was the focus on Jewish education at all levels, starting with youngsters but continuing through adult life. The recommendation involved Federation taking greater [cognizance] of the financial needs of the institutions in our community, in particular, of what

*later would become the day schools, at least, Solomon Schechter. (The Hebrew Academy, of course, existed already.) As a result, Federation, which heretofore had been somewhat conservative in its funding, gradually started giving more money to Jewish education.*

The first Federation grant to the Midrasha—which had reconstituted itself as a nondenominational school, embracing all three branches of Jewish practice in the community—paved the way for Hartford Academy (formerly called the Yeshiva of Hartford) and future schools to receive Federation subsidies. During this period, as part of a national movement to improve Jewish education, a group of interested individuals met to explore the possibility of opening a school associated with the Conservative Solomon Schechter Day School Network. According to Dr. Carl Mandel, director of the Solomon Schechter Day School (SSDS) since 1997:[63]

*The educational philosophy of the founders of the school was set forth in the initial charge by the Board… 'to create a school firmly committed to the concept that children learn best when working at their own pace and motivated by success; where age-old teachings of Judaism blend with new-world culture, which gives a child a total outlook and inspires him, which provides excellence and enrichment, which pays more than lip service to the concept of parent involvement in the child's educational success and a school which is child centered and departs from traditional forms.'*[64]

SSDS opened for the 1971–1972 school year at the Emanuel with thirty-two children enrolled in the kindergarten, first, and second grades. Each year, the school added an additional grade, teachers and support staff, so that by 2007, the student body numbered two hundred and forty students in nursery through eighth grade. Over time, the school developed a full range of after school clubs and sports programs.

In 1984, the Town of West Hartford sold the Bridlepath School on Buena Vista Road to SSDS, making it possible for the school to increase its enrollment and augment its programs. By 2002, funds, primarily from the Community Capital Campaign, permitted the school to renovate and double the size of the building. Dr. Mandel believes that:

> *Although the size, location, leadership and configuration of classes have changed over the thirty-four years that the school has been in existence, SSDS's basic purpose and philosophy has not. SSDS remains a Jewish day school, connected to the Conservative movement, whose mission is to educate the whole child, intellectually, spiritually, and physically.*[65]

As part of his personal commitment to Jewish education, in 1985, Arnold C. Greenberg, then chairman of the University of Hartford's Board of Regents, and university president Stephen Joel Trachtenberg created the Maurice Greenberg Center for Judaic Studies at the University of Hartford. According to Greenberg, who endowed the Center and named it for his late father:

> *I always had a two-fold vision for the Center…One aspect I was keenly interested in was to make certain it had a strong community program so people in Greater Hartford could come onto campus and attend programs free of charge…The second aspect—a more traditional aspect—is to make it possible for students to examine the influence of Jewish history, culture and tradition on western civilization.*[66]

In addition to the exhibitions at the George J. Sherman and Lottie K. Sherman Museum of Jewish Civilization, public lectures, and special events, the Greenberg Center offers three undergraduate degrees in Judaic Studies, a minor concentration, and double majors in education and pre-cantorial studies. Courses through the Greenberg Center include Hebrew, Bible, philosophy, religious thought, literature and fieldwork on archaeological sites. In addition, the university is in the process of creating a joint master of arts in Judaic studies program with the University of Connecticut.[67]

## Social Structure

Archaeologist Richard Freund, director of the center, was preceded by Jonathan Rosenbaum, now president of Gratz College in Pennsylvania.

In the mid-1990s, Midrasha and *Beit No'ar*, a monthly high school program in the Reform synagogues, were replaced by *Yachad*, the Greater Hartford Jewish Community High School, a supplementary program designed to draw students from a broad spectrum of synagogues and provide innovative, experiential programs as well as traditional classes. Led from the beginning by Audrey Lichter, *Yachad* also gives teens from different communities the opportunity to connect in Jewish settings. New for 2006–2007 is a collaboration that allows students to join the Jewish Community Center and participate in Yachad-sponsored classes and activities there.[68]

Although discussions had begun in the late 1980s about the need for a full-time, coeducational, modern Orthodox Hebrew high school that would serve the New Haven, Hartford and Springfield communities—and would be partially supported by those Federations—it was not until 1996 that the Hebrew High School of New England (HHNE) opened in the Agudas Achim Synagogue building on North Main Street. Eighteen ninth and tenth graders from Connecticut and Massachusetts enrolled in the rigorous dual curriculum programs of Judaic Studies and secular academic

### 'This school is for anybody'
#### Hebrew High School of New England graduates first class
By Mara Dresner

From the outside, Congregation Agudas Achim in West Hartford looks like most other suburban synagogues.

Venture downstairs, however, and a vibrant community is thriving in the halls and offices below: The Hebrew High School of New England.

Founded in 1996, the Hebrew High School of New England, Agudas Achim's tenant, started with just 18 students in the ninth and tenth grades.

Today, three years later, the school is flourishing, offering classes for ninth through 12th graders. Sixty students are signed up for the coming school year.

The school has reached a special milestone—its first-ever graduation ceremony is Monday, June 14—with eight seniors (four boys, four girls) graduating from the modern Orthodox program.

Students attend the school from Springfield, New Haven and Hartford Coun-

CLASS OF 1999 - Back row, from left, Boris Kovalevsky, Shaun Gruenbaum, Moshe Naiditch, and Rabbi Zvi Kahn. Front row, from left, Dena Weinberg, Rebecca Rosen, and Elana Freund. Missing from photo are Rachel Berman and Yitzchok Kashnow.
Photo by Richard Sweet

since the beginning. "A major highlight has been communities sincerely worked together and that is relaxed.

In one of the offices, a

courses. Underlying the entire program was a basic Jewish moral and ethical structure with its emphasis on service, *tsedakah*, and living as Jews within the community.

Rabbi Zvi Kahn, the first principal, was succeeded by Rabbi Daniel Lowe, the school's former director of Jewish Studies. In little over a decade, the school had become a four-year high school with challenging curricula in both Jewish and secular studies and by 2006 had graduated more than a hundred and seventy students.[69] As the school population has grown, the need for a new facility has become acute, and in April 2006, HHNE opened a $6 million capital campaign to finance a new structure.

## Organizations as Social Structure

The multiplicity of organizations that frequently bring people from the outer suburbs to West Hartford to share common interests is another aspect of the Jewish social structure. Not only does each synagogue provide a variety of committees and clubs, based upon age or interest, but the Federation has a number of divisions and sub-groups which raise funds and provide educational and social events. So also do the boards, auxiliaries, and committees of the beneficiary agencies. Beyond that are the local chapters of national organizations. The oldest in Greater Hartford is B'nai B'rith, a fraternal organization founded in New York in 1843. The Hartford chapter, the Ararat Lodge, opened in 1851 and became the model for later Hartford groups. According to Rabbi Morris Silverman:

> *This unique organization not only served as a center for the social, cultural and philanthropic endeavors of early Jewish settlers, but it also served as the prototype of the later Blue Cross, unemployment compensation, sick benefits and life-insurance companies established throughout this country.*[70]

Among the many national organizations with Hartford chapters—both past and present—which link local Jews to the national and international Jewish communities are the National Council of Jewish Women, the Zionist Organization of America, the Brandeis Women's Committee, the Anti-Defamation League and the fraternal orders such as the Masons and the Princess Rebekah Lodge. Jim Tierney is active in the Jewish War Veterans, which was founded in the early 1930s by World War I veterans. Said Jim:

> *I am a past post commander of Hartford, Laurel Post #45 of the Jewish War Veterans of the United States of America, as well as the*

"The normal thing like parades we're involved in. We're also working in consonance with other veterans organizations. The latest we've been involved in—not as the Jewish War Veterans but individual members—is the Connecticut Veterans Memorial in West Hartford. I was the Chairman, and a number of our Jewish War Veterans were members of the Committee." —Jim Tierney

*past department commander of the Jewish War Veterans within the state of Connecticut. We have approximately three hundred people. The Jewish War Veterans was initially put together in 1896 in response by Civil War veterans to the canard that Jews did not fight.*

*We are in the process of supporting the troops in Iraq and Afghanistan by sending care packages with those things that are not readily available: candies, salamis, cashew nuts. We have been involved in running the bingo games at the State Rocky Hill Home and Hospital. Plus we have been involved in running essay contests at Solomon Schechter and the Hebrew Academy on the topic of "What Memorial Day Means To Me." Another item that our Post has been involved in at the Jewish Community Center is in terms of security. There's an outdoor playground, and this was open to the public* [view from the street]. *The Jewish War Veterans purchased trees and planted them, and now you don't even notice the children. They're no longer a target.*

*On an annual basis, there is a Holocaust memorial at the State Capitol and the Senate Chambers. Part of it is that the Jewish War Veterans are invited to bring in the colors. This in turn recognizes the Jews' contribution in the liberation of the camps at the end of World War II. Our purpose is projecting the image of the Jewish* [war veteran] *as an integral part*

# Jewish West Hartford

Hadassah Ladies, 1930: *First Row* (left to right): Mrs. Henry Kone, Mrs. Victoria Rappaport, Mrs. Anna Hoffenberg, Mrs. Samuel Gelber and Mrs. J.R.N. Cohen. *Back Row:* Rebecca Feldman, Mrs. Elias Falk, Mrs. Sophie Hurwitz, Mrs. Hershman, Mrs. Fannie Levine, Mrs. Neiditz and Mrs. Yellin.

Social Structure

In 1990, past Hadassah presidents honor Simme Miller for twenty-six years of chairing the thrift shop. (Standing left to right) Edith Gittleman, Thelma Myerson, Bernice Veroff, Brenda Johnston, Bernice Waldman, Emma Pahuskin, Selma Stein and Faith Helene. (Back row) Ruth Sweedler, Lois Sheketoff and Anne Greenspon. (Seated) Selma Lane, Simme Miller, and Ellen Roth, Chapter President. Susan Miller, foreground.

*of our armed forces and making possible the freedom of religion within West Hartford.*

Phyllis Tierney supports Hadassah, the Women's Zionist Organization of America, whose members have helped develop and finance heath care, education and youth programs in Israel since 1912.

*I am firmly convinced that every Jewish woman should be a member of Hadassah because their projects in Israel are really great. First of all, we are so proud of those two Hadassah hospitals. They are on the cutting edge of all technology. They take care of everyone regardless of religious affiliation—that means Jews, Muslims and Christians, equal treatment for everyone. The other function is Youth Aliyah, which started out as a rescue for Jewish children in Europe. Today they take care of children in trouble. They have villages, and they're very protective of children who come from homes that can't protect them.*

*Our membership is between a thousand and twelve hundred. We meet at the Emanuel. It started out as the Hartford Chapter, but it's made up of women from West Hartford.* [All the social events are] *fundraising because that's what Hadassah does. After I served as president for two years, I became a fundraiser, which is a much harder job. I would have an annual summer luncheon. We would make the food so we spent nothing. Everything coming in was pure profit. I had a number of card parties. Sometimes the food wasn't so good, but the money was very good. Then I decided to have a theater party at the Park Road Playhouse. First of all, it was great combination. It's Hadassah, stem-cell research, and Wendy Wasserstein. Who can resist all of that and desserts by David Glass which he contributed and music by Sam Pascoe. We made three thousand dollars.*

## Jewish Businesses as Community Institutions

In addition to the religious, social service, and educational agencies and the clubs and organizations which underlie Jewish life in West Harford, three commercial ventures depend upon the Jewish population for their livelihoods and provide important services to the community: the *Jewish Ledger*, the weekly newspaper; the Crown Market, a supermarket with a large selection of kosher foods; and the Judaica Store, a shop specializing Jewish and Israeli religious and secular merchandise.

## *The Jewish Ledger*
## An Independent Weekly Newspaper Since 1929

Berthold Gaster, a young newspaperman, arrived in Hartford in 1958 at the invitation of Fred Neusner to become the managing editor of the *Jewish Ledger*. Over the years, putting out the paper became a family affair, with Gaster's wife, Adele, writing arts and entertainment reviews, covering stories and doing the layout and their son reporting on sports and Jewish athletes.

When Samuel Neusner—Fred's father and one of the paper's founders—died in 1960, Lee B. Neusner took over as publisher until 1966 when she sold the *Ledger* to Gaster and Shirley W. Bunis, the business manger. Although Rabbi Abraham Feldman of Congregation Beth Israel was co-founder and co-owner of the paper, he focused exclusively on writing editorials until his death in 1977.[71] According to Berthold Gaster:

*The* Ledger *was founded by the late Sam Neusner in April 1929 as a monthly in Springfield, although it also covered the Hartford area and quickly became a weekly. Right after that came the Depression, but* [they] *persevered and kept pushing the paper through. Then, during the war, with the shortage of newsprint and the shortage of advertising—because there wasn't very much to sell—the paper really hit hard times. Sam Neusner worked at night to make ends meet, but he kept the paper going, and I think it served a very important function through the years, as it does now.*

*We hadn't planned to buy* [the Ledger]. *In the fall of 1966, Mrs.* [Neusner] *had succeeded her husband as publisher, and she was looking to retire. She had made a deal to sell the paper to an out-of-state publisher. The deal fell through. When it did, we decided that we weren't going to let some outsider come in who didn't have any roots in the community. No matter what it took, we felt that it was important that we bought the paper. So there we were with the property, with the bills and the heartaches and also the advantages of being able to do what we wanted to within the limits of our financial ability to do it. One of our problems has been over the years was that everybody tells us what a great job we're doing, but not everybody backs it with advertising. But to put the full story in sometimes means reaching into our pockets and adding more pages to that particular week's edition. You don't get rich in this business.*

*We are the voice of the community because through our editorials we can call upon people to act. We can respond to things. We can be seen and heard by political leaders, by government leaders. We are a listening post for our readers who tell us what they are looking for, what their problems are. We try to interpret for people. We have a very intelligent, sophisticated readership. We always have to be one step ahead. But defining the problems of Israel or Soviet Jewry or the changing situation in the American-Jewish community— the problems of assimilation or the problem of what Yochim* [sic] *Prince called "survival under freedom"—I think that this is our role.*[72]

After Berthold Gaster's death in 1992, the Jewish Media Group of Miami, Florida bought the *Ledger* and appointed Jonathan Tobin, who had worked in public relations in New York, as editor, and Lisa Lenkiewicz, the former editor of the *Washington Jewish Week*, as managing editor. Among the changes were a shift to tabloid size and the computerization of production. The *Ledger* offices, which had been above Crown Market, moved within Bishop's Corner, and then to bigger offices at 924 Farmington Avenue. A few years later, the *Ledger* relocated back to the Waldbaum's quadrant of Bishop's Corner. In 1993, N. Richard Greenfield, one of the Miami investors, purchased the *Ledger* and when Tobin left in 2000, took on the responsibility of writing the editorials. Lisa Lenkiewicz remained as the lead editor.[73] She said:

## Social Structure

*People want to open up a Jewish newspaper and feel good. They want to see all of the good works that they are doing. They want to hear about their neighbors. They want to see the awards. When I go out speaking, I find that the most popular part of the paper is the obituary pages. They want to see the engagements, the weddings and the life-cycle events. It's that insular feeling of community that they are interested in.*[74]

# The Crown Market
# 2471 Albany Avenue

Even though the Edwards supermarket chain competed briefly in the early 1990s with a kosher meat department and prepared foods deli and the Bishops Corner Waldbaum's Food Mart maintains glatt kosher meat and bakery departments, the Crown Market—owned and managed by the founders and their descendants for more than sixty years—is unique. Closed on Shabbat and the Jewish holidays, the Crown stocks a large selection of packaged kosher products—particularly at Passover—and features in-house kosher meat and bakery departments and a deli which offers, among many other choices, hot pastrami, various kinds of lox and tuna salad plus all of the salads and pickles necessary for a picnic at home or at the beach. A more recent innovation, the Five O'Clock Shop, prepares about forty kosher dishes a day, with the choices ranging from traditional noodle kugels to gourmet salmons. Alan Smith, who retired from the Crown about 1990, recalls the early days of the store in Hartford and its move to West Hartford.[75]

> *The original founders of the Crown Market in 1939 were my father, Sam Smith, and Uncle Sam Sowalsky and another uncle, Meyer Goldfield. Supermarkets themselves only started in the thirties, and the concept of a kosher supermarket was not only novel, it was unique. They proceeded to acquire a piece of land on Albany Avenue between Magnolia Street and Irving Street and built a small building. It was really a group of concessions that were operated in the store. The meat and the delicatessen department were operated by the founders. The original bakery was a concession, and I believe one of the Lassoffs had the original bakery there. The fish department was Hymie Goldfarb. The fruit department was Bob Kotik and the grocery department was operated by the Winer family. About 1942 or 1943, Meyer Goldfield left the partnership and was replaced by Jack Sloat, Bill's father. The three of them continued with the operation until 1966.*

The Crown Market.

Crown Owners, 1983 (left to right) Ralph Seltzer, Marvin Cremer, William Sloat and Alan Smith.

# Social Structure

*The real breakthrough concerned the kosher meat and poultry business. For the first time you had western meat, like steers, being introduced as kosher meet. Prior to this, all your local butchers sold cow meat. This was a tremendous departure. A second departure was the fact that the cases were filled with meat that was sliced already. The third departure had to wait for the arrival of Jack Sloat. That was the concept of federally inspected New York dressed poultry. Poultry had always been bought in poultry stores, and you paid for plucking the chicken. They weighed it with blood and feathers. All of a sudden these chickens were dressed and in the case, and you picked what you wanted.*

*They added onto the Albany Avenue property, first on the east side of the store, then the west side until by the early sixties they occupied the entire block. The Crown continued on Lower Albany Avenue, expanding until 1967 when it was no longer feasible to maintain a store in an area that their clientele did not live in. When a store became available in Bishops Corner, Crown moved. At that point, Crown no longer had any operating concessions. The entire operation was run by the owners.*

*Then, the next generation came into the business. The significant innovation of the West Hartford Store was the shift into pre-packaged kosher meats. This was something that we had very great reservations about. We did not know if it would be accepted. Thank goodness it was. We opened up in West Hartford in 1967, and in 1970 we were burned out. There was fire, and the inside of the store was damaged, and the whole place was condemned for close to six weeks. Well, the flames were lapping at the back of the store; the smoke was rising through the store. We were clearing everyone out of the store except one woman at the front of the deli. "Please leave. The store is on fire. Please leave." "But I have the next number."*

*Many times I feel that Crown has evolved over the years into—yes—a business institution, but also a community institution. The community, to a certain extent, depends upon the Crown for its kosher products and accepts no excuses for not getting it. But it's also a source of Jewish information. It's amazing when the holiday comes, how many calls come into the store: When does the holiday begin? What is this holiday? What do you do for this holiday?*

By 1990, the second-generation owners were Ralph Seltzer, William Sloat and Marvin Cremer.[76] Fifteen years later, Mark Seltzer represents the third generation, with Bill Sloat and his daughter-in-law, Erin, as the owners.[77]

Inside the Judaica Store on South Whitney Street in Hartford. "What a job to clean that place! We threw out things that didn't belong to the store. In the basement was water. It was awful. The first three months, I hired Mr. Sherman to really, really teach me the business. He taught me about the people, the suppliers. He introduced me. Seven years I had that business on South Whitney." —Rivka Weiselfish

## The Judaica Store
## 31 Crossroads Plaza

When Rivka Weiselfish arrived in Hartford in 1971, it never occurred to her that one day she would own the Israel Gift Shop/Hebrew Book Store where she shopped for Hebrew records for her children. Over the years, owners Joe and Grace Sherman, who had moved to South Whitney Street from Albany Avenue when the neighborhood changed, retired and sold the store to an Israeli who lost it as part of a court case. At that point in 1988, Rivka and Susan Walpoe, a friend from her days as a Hebrew teacher, opened under the name the Judaica Store. When Susan left the business, Marla Cohen became Rivka's assistant. Seven years later, Rivka was ready to move from the Hartford location.

> I said, "I'm going only to Bishops Corner. This is the heart of the Jewish population. That's where I want to be." And we found the store, a pizza place, Dino's. When I took the store over, you could count the Judaica

Social Structure

*Photographs courtesy of the Noah Webster House & West Hartford Historical Society.*

stores all over the United States on fingers and toes. But what happened in Judaica—I think it started like everything else after '67—there was a reviving of Jewish feeling. "I'm proud to have a nice chanukiah [menorah] in my home." "I'm proud to have a seder plate. I'm going to display it." I would say [we have] a very good mixture [of products], not just religious or just secular. Both [modern American Jews and] the religious appreciate that they have a Judaica store.

[Since 1988, Rivka has seen a number of critical changes that have impacted on her inventory.] *Intermarriage, almost every artist makes today an interfaith* ketubah [marriage contract]. *I didn't have that before. Another thing that I see as a progress is the girls wearing a* tallit [prayer shawl]. *Today there are the most beautiful* tallitot *with flowers, with ribbons. People are interested in art for their houses. I sell a lot of Jewish items for house gifts, and now there is a registry for Bar and Bat Mitzvah. Ten years ago, I had one little corner for* tsedakah [charity] *boxes. Now I have three shelves full. Mezuzahs are by far the best seller. It goes back to "I'm proud to be Jewish. I'll have it on the doorposts of my house as a symbol that you know I'm Jewish."*

*My husband* [Jacob Weiselfish] *helps me with the website which is called Jacob's Ladder Judaica. Right now I am very, very comfortable* [with the store] *just the way it is, but with a lot of new merchandise all the time. If people walk in the door three times, I try very hard to memorize their names. I live in this community, and I love this community.*

## Making a Living

How West Hartford's Jews make a living has always ranged from the top of the economic ladder—leaders of corporations with international interests—to the bottom—cleaning ladies (some with degrees from foreign universities) working in private homes. To list all of the occupations would read like a telephone book: accountants to youth service providers with everything in between. Over all, those practicing the building trades—plumbers, electricians, carpenters—have been succeeded by their children who have moved into white-collar jobs. Professionals—doctors, dentists, lawyers, computer engineers, teachers—have proliferated. Some live in West Hartford and work elsewhere, others the reverse, and a third group lives and works in town. Some businesses have prospered, others have closed, still others have changed over the years or left the area. In 1966, the West Hartford Zoning office photographed many of the town businesses. Among them were these owned by Jews.

## Social Structure

## JEWISH POLITICAL LIFE

Official Jewish involvement in Hartford politics began in 1860 when Alexander Rothschild and Marcus Herlitscheck were elected to the Hartford City Council. In his *History of Hartford Jews: 1659–1970*, Rabbi Morris Silverman lists hundreds of Greater Hartford Jews, including dozens from West Hartford, who served the public in various official capacities during those years.[78] Clearly, Jews were interested in being part of the political process in America.

Although he was born in Hartford in 1890, Joseph M. Freedman was one of the first Jews to become involved in the West Hartford political life. According to Silverman:

> *From 1931 to 1934, he served on the Zoning Board of West Hartford and from 1934 to 1939, on the Zoning Appeals Board. For over twenty-five years he was a member of the Seventh District Republican Committee and secretary of the Republican Town Committee and its chairman in 1954. Joseph M. Freedman was vice-president of the West Hartford Town Council from 1947 to 1949, and when the title "mayor" was introduced, he was the first so designated, and served from 1949 to 1951...Active in the Jewish community, he was chairman of the board of directors of the Hebrew Home for the Aged.*[79]

Freedman was also the only Jewish West Hartford mayor who was a Republican. By mid-century, as the town continued to expand and change, the political structure with its influx of Democrats to the new neighborhoods had begun to shift. In the South End, which was largely Catholic, voters were encouraged to register by Katherine Quinn, who worked with state Democratic chairman John Bailey. In the North End, Harry H. Kleinman, chairman of the town Democratic Party, was instrumental in bringing the Jewish votes.[80] Kleinman, an attorney and Jewish community activist, had been a campaign worker for Franklin D. Roosevelt in the 1930s.

The second Jewish mayor was Democrat Sandra F. Klebanoff (1989–1995), followed by Nan Glass and Jonathan Harris. Over the years, as Jews settled into West Hartford, many have served the town, state and federal governments in both elected and appointed positions. Although Joan Kemler never held a town office, she represented West Hartford voters at the state level in the 1970s and 1980s. She came to Hartford from New Haven in 1951 when she married R. Leonard Kemler, and seven years later moved to West Hartford where her husband, a surgeon, was active at the Emanuel.

**KEMLER**
**TREASURER**
Vote Republican

*Proven Leadership for Connecticut!*

*Photograph courtesy of Joan Kemler.*

*I was really more involved in the greater community than I was in the synagogue. I became a member of League of Women Voters the first week I was in town. I was also very active in the Community Council. It was affiliated with the Community Chest then, the United Way. The Community Council evaluated the programs and the effectiveness of the agencies and made decisions regarding their funding.*

# Social Structure

*The League of Women Voters was pushing a state Constitutional Convention, and when the new constitution was proclaimed, the governor gave us credit for having made a valuable contribution to the process. I became very interested in state government as a result of that. The Convention was in response to the whole issue of reapportionment. That made a difference in West Hartford. We used to elect people town wide, and we now had districts for the State House of Representatives. David Neiditz, one of the legislators, lived in this district, and in 1973, David decided he would vacate his seat in the House and run for the Senate.*

*I was not the party nominee. Harry Kleinman was the chairman of the Democratic Party. He didn't really cotton to women in government, although he did like Ella* [Grasso, who became governor]. *The nominee from the West Hartford Democratic Party was a very fine person, Jeffery Mines, also of a Hartford Jewish family. I decided if I didn't challenge the nomination, it would probably be another ten years before the opportunity presented itself, so I did. I went door to door. I think the most we ever spent was maybe two thousand dollars for an election. Everything we did was done by volunteers at this table in the kitchen. We had one mailing before the election.*

*I was appointed to four committees.* [Finance, Human Services, Program Review and Appropriations] *On Appropriations they give me, as a sub-committee, the welfare budget.* [As she studied the welfare system, she realized it was not working.] *All of a sudden, the bells rang in my head, and I said I know what to do. We'll say, "We'll help you. We know you need help, but you've got to do something to help yourself." That's when I came in with legislation to have a work component in welfare. It took us two or three years to get it through. We had all kinds of things like training programs and childcare support. Using schools and education as a substitute for work, we had incentives built into it. There were a group of us who were conservative Democrats, and we're the ones who got the Workfare legislation through along with the Republicans. I was called the Wicked Witch of the West. The liberal end of the party was really gunning for me, and finally ten years later, they won by a very small margin. I can't tell you how much money they spent—thirty-five to forty thousand dollars just for a primary—and brought in people from all over the country on Election Day. We hadn't anticipated the onslaught.*

About a year after Joan Kemler's defeat by Miles Rapoport in 1984, Governor William O'Neill appointed her state treasurer to complete the remainder of Henry Parker's term, and in 1986, John Rowland—who was running in a three-way race for governor against Democrat Bruce Morrison

"I loved Harry Kleinman, a dear man, a first class rascal, and he was wonderful. He put his glasses down at the end of his nose and looked down at you. I didn't always agree with him, but I admired him tremendously. One time I was in downtown Hartford and met him on the street. We had disagreed about something in politics—I think it was when I was on the Council back in the seventies—and we stood there shouting at each other in the middle of downtown Hartford. Then we agreed to disagree." —Nan Glass

## Social Structure

Nan Glass (right) waits for the results of the West Hartford Town Council election in 1995. *Photograph courtesy of Nan Glass.*

and Independent Lowell Weicker—asked her to switch parties and run on his Republican ticket as state treasurer. Although both major parties lost to Weicker, Roland was elected four years later and named Joan Kemler to the Board of Higher Education, a position she held until her retirement eight years later.

In 1973, Democrat Nan Glass was elected to her first term on the West Hartford Town Council. During her third term, she resigned to become managing editor of the *West Hartford News*, returning to public service in 1979 to run for town clerk, a post she held until 1995 when she retired and ran again for town council. As top vote getter that year, she automatically became mayor.[81] Nan Glass never saw her religion as a factor in her political career although she believes that being Jewish shaped her social consciousness.

> *I think Judaism teaches you* [to think about] *the betterment of the world. That seems to be one of the main themes of Judaism, and one way of achieving it is economic and social equality and all those things*

*that nowadays seem unfashionable in some corners. Politics was always important in my family. My dad actually was one of Abe Ribicoff's first campaign workers way back when Abe first was elected to Congress in the forties. He became a major, major star* [as the first Jewish governor of Connecticut (1955), Secretary of Health Education and Welfare under John F. Kennedy (1961), and Connecticut's first Jewish senator (1964)]. *Abe Ribicoff was at my wedding.*

*In West Hartford you are judged according to family, education and faith. It doesn't matter if you are Jewish. It matters if you're faithful about it. Jews in West Hartford, like Jews across the country, tend to vote, tend to be interested in their government and politics and the betterment of the community. So Jewish voters lean to Jewish politicians and are contributing money. Not only did you have Jewish elected officials, you had chairmen of the party like Marilyn Cohen who was a very strong Democratic Town Chairman, very good at raising money, and yet her favorite politician was Kevin Sullivan, a good Irish boy. So that's one of the things about West Hartford. I think people just work together.*

*Jonathan Harris and Andrew Fleischmann were both classmates of my younger son at Hall High School. I am very fond of both of them. They're very good, and they do very well.* [This reflects well on the Jewish community], *of course. Andrew Fleischmann's mother was on the Board of Education. There is a long family history and the same thing with Jonathan's history. His dad, David Harris, is in the insurance field and his mother,* [Merle Harris], *in education* [as president of Charter Oak State College]. *But I don't think of them as Jewish. I think of them as good men who are working for their community. I think of Scott Slifka or Art Spada the same way, men who were devoting time to their community. Of course, Jonathan and Andrew get paid at the state level. The town people do not get paid.*

*There was a while there that Barry Feldman was town manager; Marge Wilder, the corporation council; and I was the town clerk. Sandy Klebanoff was mayor, and I began to hear rumblings in some quarters that the Jews were taking over. Sure it was a lot. Cream rises to the top, but it was so stunning to me because I think of people as people and not as a Jewish person or not a Jewish person. It was a plot to take over, you know. What are we taking over? It always just struck me as sort of odd.*

State Senator from the Fifth District and former West Hartford mayor, Jonathan Harris also comes from a family with deep roots in Hartford. His earliest memories are of growing up in the North End and of his parents'

# Social Structure

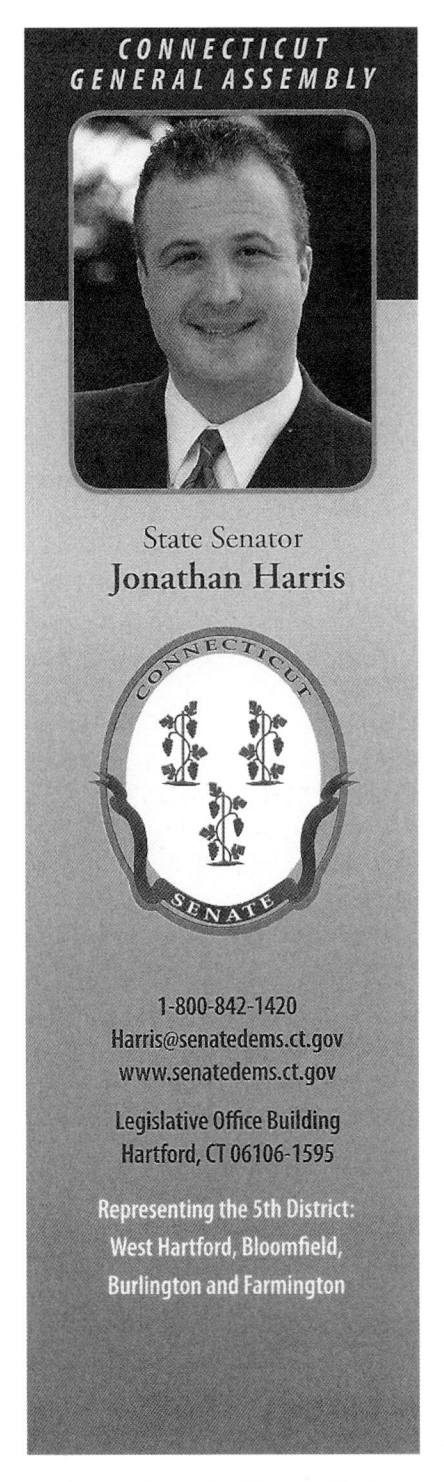

*Photograph courtesy of Jonathan Harris.*

political activities, which he attributes to their Jewish values of *tsadekah* and *tikun olum*, charity and improving the world.

> *When I was very young, my parents were involved in the Blue Hills Civic Association, which was an organization to try to keep the neighborhood together, to make sure the schools were performing, to make sure the families were staying, and it was a big thing. There was a social aspect to politics. My parents would go and be with their friends, and I would be hanging out with the kids. In 1968, my father and his friend Howard Klebanoff, whose wife* [twenty years later] *became the mayor of West Hartford, Sandy Klebanoff, bucked the Bailey regime in Hartford, and they won. When Howard ran for a second term, I remember going to the Hebrew Home with a Klebanoff poster, and we would sing, "K-L-E-B-A-N-O-F-F spells Klebanoff." Those are my first memories of politics.*
>
> *I was born in Bowles Park, a housing project, in the North End. Then my parents bought a house on Burlington Street. My parents were in that group of people to start the Solomon Schechter Day School, and I was in the first class in second grade. My sister was kindergarten. Then I went to the West Hartford schools—I think it was 1976—when we moved near Elizabeth Park, an area called Golf Acres. At one point it was part of the Hartford Golf Club.*
>
> *I graduated Hall in '82, went to Brandeis, graduated in '86. Then I worked in Washington for Barbara Kennelly, who was then Congresswoman from the First District. Then I went to New York University Law School.* [After NYU, he worked for a number of law firms, returned to West Hartford, and eventually became a political consultant and then counsel to the House Democrats in the General Assembly.]
>
> *In 2000, I decided to run against* [the longtime Republican incumbent] *Bob Farr. I knew it was an uphill battle. I worked really hard that summer. I knocked on close to six thousand doors. I would spend a couple hours every night and all day Saturday and Sunday knocking on doors for State Representative from the nineteenth district. A friend of mine ran my campaign. I raised about forty thousand dollars, and we actually won on election day by forty-three votes. The bottom line is I lost by nine votes out of twelve thousand* [in the recount]. *All I remember is all these cameras and microphones and people writing, taking notes. and I said, "What doesn't kill me makes me stronger. I trust in the process, and I have to take the bad with the good." I hugged Bob Farr and wished him luck, and I left.*
>
> *The following February, when a position opened up on the West Hartford Town Council, I was appointed, and the following year I ran*

*and became* [as top vote getter] *mayor of West Hartford. I ran in 2003, and I was mayor again. When Governor Rowland had to resign, Lieutenant Governor Rell became governor. And Kevin Sullivan, who had been the former mayor of West Hartford but had been in the Senate seat since 1986, was elevated to lieutenant governor. We opened up that seat, and I ran against a good friend and a good public servant who had been on the council for ten years, Kevin Connors.*

*When I'm with Jewish groups, they're my* landsmen [from my community of origin], *my* mispocha [family], *but I view myself as representing all the people of my community. Because of the immigration experience and my grandfather who ran for mayor of Hartford in the thirties and was blacklisted because he was a Socialist, there is a certain amount of pride in coming to West Hartford and being able to be a leader in the community. I don't think of it in terms of culture or religion oftentimes, but some of that's there. The important part is the idea of community involvement, the idea of* tikun olam, *social justice, all the things I was raised to think about. Those fuel what I do every day. So, am I a Jewish mayor or a Jewish senator? No, but by the same token, I am, because those are the values I've been brought up with.*

## OVER THE LINE IN BLOOMFIELD

Bloomfield—at one time home to many Jews—hosts three institutions that draw West Hartford residents. The oldest, Tumble Brook Country Club on Simsbury Road, opened in 1922 with a clubhouse and nine-hole golf course. Although it had originated in the German Jewish Truro Club, membership eventually opened to Jews from all backgrounds.[82] With many of the members serving as organizers of and contributors to the Jewish charities, Tumble Brook has always been closely, if unofficially, affiliated with the Federation. Not only were many Tumble Brook members presidents and campaign chairmen of the Federation, but the building itself was the frequent site of Federation gatherings, both formal and informal, and members were required to support the community, particularly the Federation, financially.

The second institution to move to Bloomfield from Hartford's North End was Congregation Tikvoh Chadoshoh—New Hope—which built its new building on Still Road in 1969. The congregation, founded in 1942 by those fleeing from Germany and Austria, was led by Rabbi Hans Bodenheimer, himself a refugee, who preached in German. Although the congregation used the German Orthodox prayer book and printed its newsletter in that language for many years, recently Tikvoh Chadoshoh has grown to include Jews of all backgrounds and has adopted more mainstream Conservative practices. Today Lilly Kaufman serves as rabbi and cantor.

Even though most of the Jews had moved out of the city by the middle 1960s, supporters of the Yeshiva of Hartford were determined to stay in their newly renovated building on Cornwall Street, but a fire in 1965 and a robbery in 1970 convinced them to relocate to Bloomfield. In 1974, the new building on Gabb Road was dedicated and in 1979 the Yeshiva renamed the Bess and Paul Sigel Hebrew Academy.[83] The Orthodox school, which offers pre-school through eighth grade classes, strives to provide "the highest level of Judaic and General education to children and families of all affiliations in the community, and to develop Jews who are proud of their heritage, involved in their community and devoted to G-d, Torah and *Klal Yisrael* (the Jewish people.)"[84]

✡

*Basically, I really like West Hartford. To me it's very small town. People said to me, "Oh, you'll never be able to break into cliques." and "People who grew up here, they tend to stay together." and "You're an outsider. You're a newcomer, and you're not going to fit in, and they won't accept you." Maybe I'm the exception, but I found that I did make friends basically because of my activities. I got involved with the synagogue and Sisterhood and activities there so I never felt that this was a problem. I found people very nice, and I kind of enjoyed the fact that in* [contrast to] *New York where my mother lived in an apartment building for twenty years and never knew anybody but one neighbor, here I go to the supermarket, and I can't get through the supermarket because I'm stopping and talking to so many people. I think that's a very nice feature of the town.*[85]

—Marsha Lotstein

# Notes

## Introduction

1. Butterworth, Miriam, Ellsworth Grant and Richard Woodworth. *Celebrate! West Hartford: An Illustrated History*. West Hartford: CWH, LLC, 2001.
2. Silverman, Morris. *Hartford Jews: 1659–1970*. Hartford: The Connecticut Historical Society, 1970.
3. Ibid.
4. Dalin, David G. and Jonathan Rosenbaum. *Making a Life: Building a Community: A History of the Jews of Hartford*. New York/London: Holmes & Meier, 1997.
5. Silverman. 1970. Ellsworth Grant and Marion Grant, *The City of Hartford, 1784–1984*. Hartford: Connecticut Historical Society, 1986; Betty Hoffman. *Jewish Hearts: A Study of Dynamic Ethnicity in the United States and the Soviet Union*. Albany: SUNY Press, 2001.

## Chapter One

6. Butterworth et al, 2001.
7. In 2006 Stanley Weisen compiled a list of more than sixty builders, most of them Jewish. It is on file at the JHSGH.
8. Butterworth et al, 2001.
9. Blitzer, Jessica. Interview with Marsha Lotstein. West Hartford Historical Society, 2004.
10. Hirsch, Linda B. "West Hartford: A town divided." *Hartford Courant*. September 29, 1993.
11. Blitzer, 2004.

## Chapter Two

12. Rafal, Marjorie L. *The Way We Were: 1843–2001*. West Hartford: Congregation Beth Israel, 2001.
13. Feldman, Abraham J. "A Modern Synagogue: A description of Congregation Beth Israel" in Rafal, 2001.
14. Cohen, Rabbi William in unidentified newspaper clipping.
15. www.bethdavidwh.org
16. Teferes Israel Anshe Russia and the Chevre Kadishe, which had both been founded in 1906 in Hartford, merged in 1926 into a single synagogue incorporating both names. In 1970, the congregation, led by Rabbi Haskel Lindenthal, moved to Bloomfield under the simplified name of Teferes Israel. Four years later, Chevry Lumday Mishnayes, which was disbanding, donated everything from the synagogue to Teferes Israel. In 1993, when Rabbi Lindenthal retired, Teferes Israel merged with Beth David. (Dalin and Rosenbaum, 1997).
17. Jonathan S. Tobin, "An Orthodox centrist: Rabbi Adler to teach and reach out at Beth David," Ledger.
18. Kemler, R. Leonard. "History of the Emanuel," The Emanuel at 70, 1919–1989, anniversary booklet, 1989.
19. Dalin and Rosenbaum, 1997.
20. Ibid.
21. www.bethelwesthartford.org
22. http://www.emanuelsynagogue.org/Default.aspx?fusemode=COC

## Chapter Three

23. Gaster, Berthold. Interviewer, JHSGH, 1978.
24. www.jewishhartford.org/synagogues
25. Personal communication, February 1, 2007.
26. Gaster interview with Rabbi Abraham N. AvRutick. June 19, 1974.
27. AvRutick, Rabbi Abraham N., GHJHS speech, March 8, 1978.
28. Personal communication, February 1, 2007.
29. Trencher, Mark and Sherry Haller, "A History of Young Israel of West Hartford" unpublished manuscript, updated 2006.
30. Gelb, Sally. "History of the Young Israel of Hartford in West Hartford," unpublished manuscript, February 2007.
31. http://en.wikipedia.org/wiki/Chabad and www.chabadhartford.com
32. Personal communication with Phil Schlossberg. February 21, 2007.
33. "Henry Levy to be interviewed by the Historical Society." *Hartford Jewish Ledger*, December 11, 1980.
34. Levy, Madalyn in a letter to Henry Levy, June 27, 1995, JHSGH Sephardic file.
35. Levy, Henry. *Hartford Jewish Ledger*, 1980 and Dresner, Stacy, "Voices of the Sephardim," *Hartford Jewish Ledger*, November 13, 1992.

36. Personal communication. Madalyn Levy, February 18, 2007.
37. Personal communication.

## Chapter Four

38. Hoffman, Betty N. *Honoring the Past: Building the Future: The History of the Jewish Federation of Greater Hartford*. Hartford: JHSGH 2007.
39. Certificate of Organization of the Hartford Jewish Federation, 1945, on file at the JHSGH.
40. Hoffman, Betty, interview with Paula Steinberg, October 11, 2004, quoted in Hoffman, 2007.
41. Hartford Jewish Federation, Report, 1948–1949.
42. Silverman, 1970.
43. Celebrating 80: 1915—1595. The Greater Hartford Jewish Community Center. Dalin and Rosenbaum 1997.
44. *Hartford Courant*. December 29, 1977.
45. Lucy Dratva translated for Lazar Grabarnik, Mark Aronov, and Mayya Patent, November 14, 2006.
46. Celebrating 80, 1995.
47. Dalin and Rosenbaum, 1997.
48. Silverman, 1970.
49. "Htfd. Community Asked to Take 100 Soviet Jews," *Ledger*.
50. http://www.jfshartford.org/histmission.htm
51. *Ledger*, September 9, 1977.
52. *Ledger*, September 5, 1976.
53. "Mikveh Bess Israel Undergoing Renovations with Burial Society Aid" *Ledger*, March 8, 1984.
54. Due to federal regulations, the land which Simon Konover had offered to donate to the community had a market value that put it outside the limits for a Section 202 property. HUD suggested that he develop the property under Section 8 for profit housing and allow the social service agencies to provide services to the tenants, which he did. Said Robert J. Fishman, the Federation staff member who wrote the original proposal, "In other words, the community was out of the project. In his generosity he decided it should be called Federation Square even though it's not owned by the Federation."
55. Marlene Scharr, "Federation's Newest Agency: Jewish Community Living", *Community Voice*, February 25, 1982.
56. "JCL…New Beginning," *Community Voice*, January 20, 1983.
57. Silverman, 1970 and Alderman. "The Formation of the Hartford Federation of Jewish Philanthropies: A Reflection of the Hartford Jewish Community: 1880–1980, (JHSGH, unpublished paper).
58. Sandy Zieky and Judy Greenberg, *Promises Kept, Celebration Program*. Hebrew Home and Hospital, 1989; Silverman, 1970.
59. Zieky and Greenberg, 1989.

60. "Hebrew Home & Hospital Building Project Reflects Future Needs," *Community Voice*, March, 1986.
61. Zieky and Greenberg, 1989.
62. "Community Capital Campaign Moves Forward," FYI, Winter 1999.

## Chapter Five

63. Previous principals were Ruth Weiner and Fred Nathan (who also taught classes), Daniel Grossberg (the school's first full time principal), Moshe Zwang, Mervyn Danker and Carl Mandell.
64. Carl Mandel, "Solomon Schechter School History," e-mail to the author. September 19, 2005.
65. Ibid.
66. Judie Jacobson, *Ledger*, 10/28/2005.
67. www.hartford.edu/greenberg/programs.asp
68. www.yachad.net
69. http://www.hhne.org/index.php?pgid=10
70. Silverman, 1970.
71. Dahlin and Rosenbaum, 1997.
72. Interview by Morris N. Cohen, Jewish Historical Society of Greater Hartford, December 8, 1977, addedndum, 1/7/1978.
73. Personal commuication. January 7, 1978.
74. Interview with Luke Ford, June 24, 2004. http://www.lukeford.net/profiles/profiles/lisa_lenkiewicz.htm
75. Interview with Alan Smith, JHSGH, May 12, 1983.
76. Linda Giuca, *Courant* Food Editor, "Crown owners make store a family affair," December 12, 1990.
77. Personal communication with Erin Sloat, February 23, 2007.
78. Silverman, 1970.
79. Ibid.
80. Butterworth et al, 2001.
81. Ibid.
82. Silverman, 1970.
83. Leon Chameides, *Teach them Diligently to your Children: A History of the Bess and Paul Sigel Hebrew Academy of Greater Hartford*, unpublished manuscript.
84. http://www.sigelacademy.org/missionstatement.shtml
85. Blitzer, 2004.

# About the Author

Anthropologist Betty N. Hoffman, PhD, has conducted research in central Connecticut in conjunction with the Jewish Historical Society of Greater Hartford and the Noah Webster House/West Hartford Historical Society for more than twenty years. Her varied academic career includes teaching English as a second language, academic and business writing, and anthropology and social science research methods at various local universities. Her oral history and anthropology publications include *Honoring the Past: Building the Future: The History of the Jewish Federation of Greater Hartford* (JHSGH, 2007), *Jewish Hearts: A Study in Dynamic Ethnicity in the United States and the Soviet Union* (SUNY Press, 2001), and "Witness to War: 1941–1945: The Soviet Jewish Experience" *Connecticut Jewish History* (JHSGH, 2001). She is president of the New England Association for Oral History.

Visit us at
www.historypress.net